LEARN C PROGRAMMING

C PROGRAM PRACTICAL'S ONLY

AVINASH NANASAHEB PAGAR

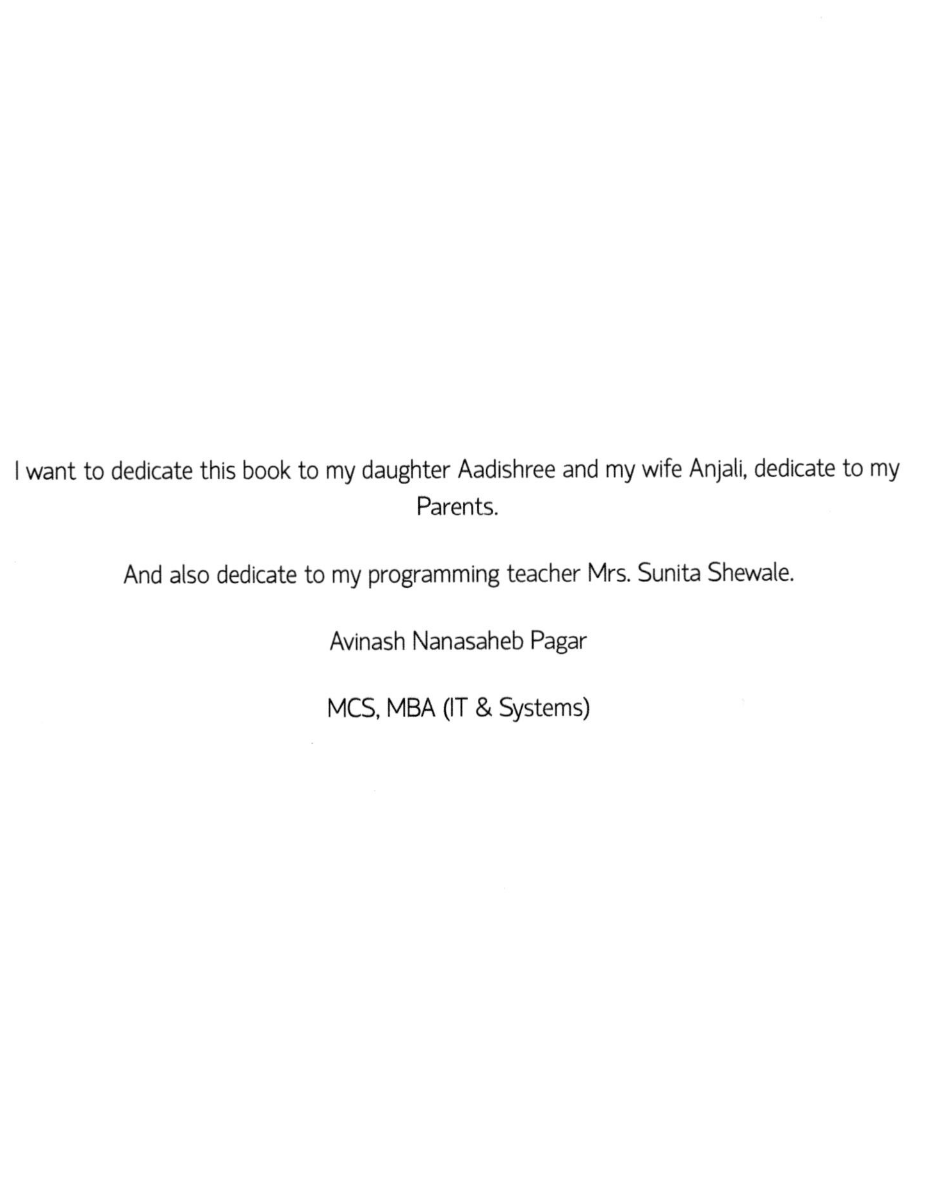

I want to dedicate this book to my daughter Aadishree and my wife Anjali, dedicate to my Parents.

And also dedicate to my programming teacher Mrs. Sunita Shewale.

Avinash Nanasaheb Pagar

MCS, MBA (IT & Systems)

Contents

CHAPTER ONE

Introduction

Basic Programmes

P -1] Welcome to C.

P -2] Addition of two number's.

P -3] Average of two integers data type number's.

P -4] Perform arithmetic operation +, -, * and /.

P -5] Convert given temprature from Farenheit degree into Centigrade degree.

P -6] Accept distance between two cities in km and display into meter, feet, inches and centimeters.

P -7] Calculate area of Circle.

P -8] Calculate area of Square.

P -9] Calculate area of Rectangle.

P -10] Calculate area of Triangle.

P -11] Calculate area and volume of Sphere.

P -12] Calculate area of a Polygon with the length 2 and the number of side is 4.

P -13] Calculate area of a kite with the given diagonals 2,4 using diagonal method.

P -14] Calculate Roots of quadratic equation ax2+bx+c.

P -15] Print Student Marksheet.

P -16] Calculate a Simple Interest.

P -17] Calculate the sum of first and last digits 4 digit no.

P -18] Swap value of A & B using temporary variable.

P -19] Swap value of A & B without temporary variable.

P -20] Swap two values using bitwise.

P -21] Swap two values using pointers.

P -22] Check whether entered character is vowel or not.

P -23] Find Absolute value of given number.

P -24] Calculate value of tan.
p- 25] Print Round up value of given number using Celi function.
P -26] Perform use of atof()
P -27] Calculate value of cos.
P -28] Printf current date & time – Type 1.
P -29] Display Round down value of given no using floor function.
P -30] Printf date & time – Type 2
P -31] Print log value of given no.
P -32] Calculate sqare root of given no.
P -33] Calculate value of Log base 10.
P -34] Calculate value of sin.
P -35] Calculate Power of value.
P -36] Calculate Power 10 value of given no.
P -37] Rename file name.
P -38] Change textcolor of text.
P -39] Perform Blinking text function.
P -40] Close program after particular time interval.
P -41] Change cursor position.
P -42] Display cursor vertical position.
P -43] Use of KBHIT() function.
P -44] Remove directory from bin directory.
P -45] Change text background color.
P -46] Display horizontal cursor position.
P -47] Check alphanumeric characters.
P -48] Check digits or not.
P -49] Calculate gross salary.
P -50] Calculate sum of digit.
P -51] Print reverse number.
P -52] Calculate total number of illiterate Boys and Girls.
P -53] Calculate total no. Of Currency Notes of each denomination.
P -54] Read & Write string.
P -55] Calculate square and cube of number after & previos no.
P -56] Fiil entire screen with spade.
P -57] Calculate average of two float data type number's.
P -58] Calculate Area of Circle using a math.h header file.

If Statement Programs

P -59] Check whether given no is even or odd.
P -60] Find maximum number between two number's.

Pattern Programs

P -164] Write a function power(a,b) calculate the value of a raised to b.
P -165] Calculate factorial value of an integer using a function.
P -166] Find out whether a year is leap or not using function.
P -167] Print year into its roman equivalent.
P -168] Calculate prime factors of a number.
P -169] Find prime factors of number recursively.
P -170] Find Binary equivalent of a decimal number.
P -171] Check whether vowels or not using function.
P -172] Perform Nested function operation.
P -173] Check type of shape.

C Preprocessor Programs

P -174] Macros like ISUPPER,ISLOWER,ISALPHA,BIG.
P -175] Calculate area,perimeter and circumference using macros.
P -176] Macros like MEAN,ABS,TOLOWER,BIG.

Array – One Dimensional

P -177] Find maximum no from given array.
P -178] Find smallest and largest no from 10 nos.
P -179] Calculate sum of element & average of one dimensional array.
P –180] Print one dimensional array.
P -181] Search number in single dimensional array.
P -182] Sort one dimentional array in an ascending order.
P -183] Sort one dimentional array in descending order.
P -184] Print array elements in reverse order.
P -185] Search element using linear search.
P -186] Search element using binary Search.
P -187] Insert element in array
P -188] Delete element from array.
P -189] Sorting method Bubble sort.
P -190] Sorting method Insertion sort.
P -191] Sorting method Selection sort.
P -192] Get number's find even, odd & sum of them.
P -193] Copy one array into another array in the revers order.
P -194] Computation of standard deviation.
P -195] Calculate equation of straight line.
P -196] Calculate bonus of employee salaries.
P -197] Convert binary to decimal conversion.
P -198] Convert decimal to binary conversion.
P -199] Perform Union operation on array.

P -200] Read two arrays and sort them and merge them to from a third sorted array.

P -201] Perform Intersection operation on array.

Matrix Programs - Two Dimensional Array

P -202] Print the matrix (two dimensional array)

P -203] Search number from matrix.

P -204] Perform operation addition of two matrices.

P -205] Find minimum no from two dimentional array.

P -206] Find largest no from 2*2 matrix.

P -207] Sort two dimentional array.

P -208] Print even no from two dimentional array.

P -209] Print odd no from two dimentional array.

P -210] Print prime no from two dimentional array.

P -211] Calculate matrix multiplication.

P -212] Print Transpose Of matrix

P -213] Print the upper triangular matrix.

P -214] Calculate sum of upper triangular matrix.

P -215] Find minimum no from upper triangular matrix.

P -216] Find maximum no from upper triangular matrix.

P -217] Print lower triangular matrix.

P -218] Print minimum no from lower triagular matrix.

P -219] Print maximum no from lower triagular matrix.

P -220] Calculate sum of lower triagular matrix.

P -221] Print the identity matrix.

P -222] Calculate and print sum of row elements.

P -223] Calculate and print sum of column elements.

P -224] Calculate and print sum of row and column of matrix.

P -225] Find maximum number from row of matrix.

P -226] Find maximum number from column of matrix.

P -227] Find minimum number from row of matrix.

P -228] Find minimum number from column of matrix.

P -229] Calculate determinant value of 3*3 matrix.

P -230] Check whether square matrix is symmetric or not.

P -231] Perform operaion matrix substraction.

Pointer Program

P -232] Addition of two numbers using pointer.

P -233] Search string using pointer.

P -234] Perform operations sum,average and standerd deviation using function.

P -235] Perform Pointer to pointer.

String Programs

P -236] Calculate string length using strlen() function.

P -237] Calculate string length without using strlen() function.

P -238] Compare Two Strings using strcmp.

P -239] Compare Two Strings without using strcmp.

P -240] Copy string using strcpy() function.

P -241] Concanate two strings using strcat() function.

P -242] Concanate two strings without using strcat() function.

P -243] Print reverse of given string.

P -244] Print reverse of string using recersion.

P -245] Check whether string is palindrome or not.

P -246] Remove vowels from string.

P -247] Find substring of string.

P -248] Find substring of all strings.

P -249] Sort string alphabetically.

P -250] Remove blank spaces from string.

P -251] Convert string into lowercase using strlwr() function.

P -252] Convert string into uppercase using strupr() function.

P -253] Convert string into uppercase without using strupr() function.

P -254] Convert string into lowercase without using strlwr() function.

P -255] Swap two strings.

P -256] Find occurrence of characters in string.

P -257] Print anagram.

P -258] Replace more than one blank with a single blank.

P -259] Replace a substring.

P -260] Reverse string stored in an array of pointers.

P -261] Delete all vowels from a sentence.

P -262] Delete all occurrences of "an" from a sentence.

P -263] Count the no of lowercase and uppercase alphabets.

P -264] To read a string and capatalise the first character of every word.

P -265] Determine how many characters, digits, white spaces and other kind of characters.

P -266] Program of using function read & write string.

Structure Programs

P -267] Add two complex numbers.

P -268] Create structure to store student data.

P -269] Create structure for store customers bank account detail.

P -270] Create structure to store engine parts data.

P -271] Create structure and compare the dates.

P -272] Calculate net salary using structure.

Console Program

P -273] Function getint().

File Handling Programs

P -274] Perform Read a file operation.

P -275] Perform copy file operation.

P -276] perform two files merge operation.

P -277] Display files in the current directory.

P -278] Perform file delete operation.

P -279] Display a file with line number.

P -280] Find the size of a text file.

P -281] Display the content of a file.

P -282] Read a file in binary mode and display its content.

P -283] Create a file on disk, retrive data as required.

P -284] Count total number of words in a file.

P -285] Read a text file and print each word in reverse order.

Command Line Argument Programs

P -286] Search for a word in a file and replace it with the specified word.

P -287] Perform the given arithmetic operation on the two integers.

Graphics Program

P -288] Perform draw different shapes.

P -289] Write a program to draw Bar Chart.

P -290] Write a program to create Circles in Circle.

P -291] Write a program to Draw ellipse.

P -292] Write a program to draw line.

P -293] Write a program for get Color.

P -294] Write a program to draw a circle.

P -295] Write a program to draw a arc.

P -296] Write a program to draw a bar.

P -297] Write a program to draw a polygon.

P -298] Write a program to fill polygon shape.

Windows Programs

P -299] Write a Program for gettime.

P -300]Write a Program To Display Mouse Pointer In Textmode.

P -301] Write a Program for getdate.

CHAPTER TWO

Basic Programmes

Program -1] Welcome to C.

```
#include<stdio.h>
#include<conio.h>
main()
{
clrscr();
printf("Welcome To C Programming...");
getch();
return(0);
}
```

Output:

Welcome To C Programming...

Program -2] Addition of two number's.

```
#include<stdio.h>
#include<conio.h>
main()
{
int no1,no2,ans;
clrscr();
printf("\nEnter The First Number:");
scanf("%d",&no1);
printf("\nEnter The Second Number:");
scanf("%d",&no2);
ans=no1+no2;
printf("\nAddition of %d & %d is=%d",no1,no2,ans);
// Assign a another value to the no1 & no2 And add them
```

```
no1=100;
no2=200;
printf("\n\nAfter assign a value to the no1=%d & no2=%d",no1,no2);
printf("\n\nAddition is=%d",(no1+no2));
getch();
return(0);
}
```

Input:

Enter The First Number:20

Enter The Second Number:30

Output:

Addition of 20 & 30 is=50

After assign a value to the no1=100 & no2=200

Addition is=300

Program -3] Average of two integer data type Number's.

```
#include<stdio.h>
#include<conio.h>
main()
{
int a,b;
clrscr();
printf("Enter first number:");
scanf("%d",&a);
printf("Enter second number:");
scanf("%d",&b);
printf("Average of %d & %d is=%f",a,b,(float)(a+b)/2);
getch();
return(0);
}
```

Input:

Enter first number:4

Enter second number:6

Output:

Average of 4 & 6 is=5.00

Program -4] Program for addition, subtraction, multiplication and division of two numbers.

```
#include<stdio.h>
#include<conio.h>
void main()
{
float a,b;
float p,q,r,s;
clrscr();
printf("\n Enter any two numbers:");
scanf("%f%f",&a,&b);
p = a+b;
q = a-b;
r = a*b;
s = a/b;
printf("\nAddition is: %f",p);
printf("\nSubtraction is: %f",q);
printf("\nMultiplication is: %f",r);
printf("\nDivision is: %f",s);
getch();
}
```

Input:

Enter First number:56

Enter Second number:23

Output:

Addition is: 79.000000

Substraction is: 33.000000

Multiplication is: 1288.000000

Division is: 2.434783

Program -5] Program to convert given temperature from Fahrenheit degree into centigrade degree.

```
#include<stdio.h>
#include<conio.h>
main()
```

```
{
int f;
float c;
clrscr();
printf("\n Enter temperature in Fahrenheit:");
scanf("%d",&f);
c=0.55*(f-32);
printf("The temperature in Celsius is=%5.2f\n",c);
getch();
return(0);
}
```

Input:

Enter temperature in Fahrenheit:45

Output:

The temperature in Celsius is= 7.15

Program -6] Program to accept distance between two cities in km and it display

into meter, feet, inches and centimeters.

```
#include<stdio.h>
#include<conio.h>
main()
{
float d,m,feet,inch,cen;
clrscr();
printf("\n Enter distance between two cities in kilometers:=");
scanf("%f",&d);
m = d * 1000;
feet = d * 1000 * 3.25;
inch = d * 1000 * 39;
cen = d * 1000 * 100;
printf("\n Distance in Kilometers %0.2f\n",d);
printf("\n Distance in Meters %0.2f\n",m);
printf("\n Distance in Feet %0.2f\n",feet);
printf("\n Distance in Inch %0.2f\n",inch);
printf("\n Distance in Centimeters %0.2f\n",cen);
getch();
```

```
return(0);
}
```

Input:

Enter distance between two cities in kilometers:=1

Output:

Distance in Kilometers 1.00
Distance in Meters 1000.00
Distance in Feet 3250.00
Distance in Inch 39000.00
Distance in Centimeters 100000.00

Program -7] Calculate Area of Circle.

```
#include<stdio.h>
#include<conio.h>
main()
{
const float pi=3.14;
float r,ac;
clrscr();
printf("Enter radius of circle: ");
scanf("%f",&r);
ac=pi*r*r;
printf("\nThe area of circle is :%0.2f",ac);
getch();
return(0);
}
```

Input:

Enter radius of circle: 4

Output:

The area of circle is: 50.24

Program -8] Calculate Area of Square.

```
#include<stdio.h>
#include<conio.h>
#include<math.h>
main()
```

```
{
int side;
float ar;
clrscr();
printf("Enter side of square: ");
scanf("%d",&side);
ar=(float)pow(side,2);
printf("The area of square is: %0.2f",ar);
getch();
return(0);
}
```

Input:

Enter side of square: 4

Output:

The area of square is: 16.00

Program -9] Calculate Area of Rectangle.

```
#include<stdio.h>
#include<conio.h>
#include<math.h>
main()
{
int l,b;
float arearec;
clrscr();
printf("Enter the length :");
scanf("%d",&l);
printf("Enter the breadth:");
scanf("%d",&b);
arearec=(float)l*b;
printf("The area of rectangle is:%0.2f",arearec);
getch();
return(0);
}
```

Input:

Enter the length :4

Enter the breadth:6

Output:

The area of rectangle is:24.00

Program -10] Program to calculate Area of Triangle.

```
#include<stdio.h>
# include<conio.h>
main()
{
int p,q,r;
float a,s;
clrscr();
printf("\n Enter three side length of the triangle :");
scanf("\n%d%d%d",&p,&q,&r);
s = (p+q+r)/2;
a = sqrt(s*(s-p)*(s-q)*(s-r));
printf("Area of Triangle is :%f\n",a);
getch();
return(0);
}
```

Input:

Enter three side length of the triangle :4 4 4

Output:

Area of Triangle is :6.928203

Program -11] Program to calculate area and volume of sphere.

```
#include<stdio.h>
#include<conio.h>
main()
{
int r;
float a,v;
clrscr();
printf("\n Enter the radius of sphere:");
scanf("%d",&r);
a =(float)4*3.14*r*r*r;
v =(float)1.33*3.14*r*r*r;
```

```
printf("\nArea is :%.3f\n",a);
printf("\nVolume is :%.2f\n",v);
getch();
return(0);
}
```

Input:

Enter the radius of sphere:2

Output:

Area of sphere :100.480

Volume of sphere :33.41

Program -12] Find the area of a polygon with the length 2 and the number of side is 4.

```
#include<stdio.h>
#include<conio.h>
#include<math.h>
void main()
{
int side_lenght=2,n=4,Poly_Area;
clrscr();
Poly_Area=(pow(side_lenght,2)*n)/(4*tan(3.14/n));
printf("\nThe area of plygon is :%d",Poly_Area);
getch();
}
```

Output:

The area of polygon is :4

Program -13] Find the area of a kite with the given diagonals 2,4 using diagonal method.

```
#include<stdio.h>
#include<conio.h>
void main()
{
int d1=2,d2=4,Kite_Area;
```

```
clrscr();
Kite_Area=0.5*d1*d2;
printf("\nThe area of Kite is :%d",Kite_Area);
getch();
}
```

Output:

The area of Kite is :4

Program -14] Roots of quadratic equation ax2+bx+c.

```
#include<stdio.h>
#include<conio.h>
#include<math.h>
main()
{
int a,b,c;
float x1,x2;
clrscr();
printf("Enter the value of a=");
scanf("%d",&a);
printf("Enter the value of b=");
scanf("%d",&b);
printf("Enter the value of c=");
scanf("%d",&c);
x1=((b*b)+sqrt(4*b*c))/(2*a);
x2=((b*b)-sqrt(4*b*c))/(2*a);
printf("\nThe first root is:%0.2f",x1);
printf("\nThe second root is:%0.2f",x2);
getch();
return(0);
}
```

Input:

Enter the value of a:2

Enter the value of b:4

Enter the value of c:6

Output:

The first root is:6.45

The second root is:1.55

Program -15] Student Marksheet.

```
#include<stdio.h>
#include<conio.h>
#include<string.h>
void main()
{
int s1,s2,s3,s4,s5,s6,total;
float per;
char studname[20],grade[20];
clrscr();
printf("\nEnter student name:");
gets(studname);
printf("\nEnter the marks of six subject:");
scanf("%d%d%d%d%d%d",&s1,&s2,&s3,&s4,&s5,&s6);
total=s1+s2+s3+s4+s5+s6;
per=(float)total/6;
printf("\n\t\tResult");
printf("\n--------------------------------------");
printf("\nStudent Name:%s",studname);
printf("\n--------------------------------------");
printf("\nSubject \tMarks");
printf("\n--------------------------------------");
printf("\nSubject1\t%d",s1);
printf("\nSubject2\t%d",s2);
printf("\nSubject3\t%d",s3);
printf("\nSubject4\t%d",s4);
printf("\nSubject5\t%d",s5);
printf("\nSubject6\t%d",s6);
printf("\n--------------------------------------");
printf("\nTotal:%d",total);
printf("\nPercentage:%0.2f",per);
if(per>75)
printf("\nGrade:Distinction");
else if(per<75 && per>=60)
printf("\nGrade:First Class");
else if(per<60 && per>=50)
```

```
printf("\nGrade:Second Class");
else if(per<50 && per>=35)
printf("\nGrade:Third Division");
else
printf("\nGrade:Fail");
printf("\n--------------------------------------");
getch();
}
```

Input:

```
Enter student name:Rahul
Enter the marks of six subject:40 50 60 70 80 90
```

Output:

```
Result
--------------------------------------
Student Name:Rahul
--------------------------------------
Subject Marks
--------------------------------------
Subject1 40
Subject2 50
Subject3 60
Subject4 70
Subject5 80
Subject6 90
--------------------------------------
Total:390
Percentage:65.00
Grade:First Class
--------------------------------------
```

Program -16] Calculate a Simple Interest.

```
#include<stdio.h>
#include<conio.h>
#include<math.h>
main()
{
float p,r,SimpleInt;
```

```
int n;
clrscr();
printf("Enter the Principle Amount:");
scanf("%f",&p);
printf("Enter the Rent:");
scanf("%f",&r);
printf("Enter the no of year's:");
scanf("%d",&n);
SimpleInt=(float)((p*n*r)/100);
printf("\nThe Simple Interest is:%0.2f",SimpleInt);
getch();
return(0);
}
```

Input:

Enter the Principle Amount:20000

Enter the Rent:10

Enter the no of year's:1

Output:

The Simple Interest is:2000.00

Program -17] Program to calculate the sum of first and last digits of 4 digit no.

```
#include<stdio.h>
#include<conio.h>
main()
{
int n,a,sum=0;
clrscr();
printf("\n Enter a four digit no:");
scanf("%d",&n);
a=n/1000;
sum=sum+a;
a=n%10;
sum=sum+a;
printf("\n Sum of first and last digit of %d is=%d",n,sum);
getch();
return(0);
```

```
}
```

Input:

Enter a four digit no:1234

Output:

Sum of first and last digit of 1234 is=5

Program -18] Swap Value Of A & B. Using Temporary Variable.

```
#include<stdio.h>
#include<conio.h>
main()
{
int x, y, temp;
clrscr();
printf("Enter the value of x and y:");
scanf("%d%d",&x, &y);
printf("Before Swapping\nx = %d\ny = %d\n",x,y);
temp = x;
x = y;
y = temp;
printf("After Swapping\nx = %d\ny = %d\n",x,y);
getch();
return 0;
}
```

Input:

Enter the value of x and y:4 6

Output:

Before Swapping

x = 4

y = 6

After Swapping

x = 6

y = 4

Program -19] Swap Value Of A & B Without Temporary Variable.

```
#include<stdio.h>
#include<conio.h>
```

```
void main()
{
int a, b;
clrscr();
printf("Enter two numbers to swap:");
scanf("%d%d",&a,&b);
a = a + b;
b = a - b;
a = a - b;
printf("a = %d\nb = %d\n",a,b);
getch();
}
```

Input:

Enter two numbers to swap:4 6

Output:

a = 6

b = 4

Program -20] Swap two values using bitwise.

```
#include<stdio.h>
#include<conio.h>
void main()
{
int a, b;
clrscr();
printf("Enter two numbers to swap: ");
printf("\na=");
scanf("%d",&a);
printf("\nb=");
scanf("%d",&b);
a = a ^ b;
b = a ^ b;
a = a ^ b;
printf("\nAfter swaping the values of \na = %d\nb = %d\n",a,b);
getch();
}
```

Input:

Enter two numbers to swap:

a=4

b=6

Output:

After swaping the values of

a = 6

b = 4

Program -21] Swap two values using pointers.

```
#include<stdio.h>
#include<conio.h>
void main()
{
int x, y, *a, *b, temp;
clrscr();
printf("Enter the value of x and y:");
scanf("%d%d",&x,&y);
printf("\nBefore Swapping\nx = %d\ny = %d\n", x, y);
a = &x;
b = &y;
temp = *b;
*b = *a;
*a = temp;
printf("After Swapping\nx = %d\ny = %d\n", x, y);
getch();
}
```

Input:

Enter the value of x and y:4 6

Output:

Before Swapping

x = 4

y = 6

After Swapping

x = 6

y = 4

Program -22] Check whether enter character is Vowel or not.

```
#include<stdio.h>
#include<conio.h>
void main()
{
char ch;
clrscr();
printf("Enter a character\n");
scanf("%c",&ch);
if ( ch == 'a' || ch == 'A' || ch == 'e' || ch == 'E' || ch == 'i' || ch == 'I' || ch
=='o' || ch=='O' || ch == 'u' || ch == 'U')
printf("%c is a vowel.\n", ch);
else
printf("%c is not a vowel.\n", ch);
getch();
}
```

Input:

Enter a character:i

Output:

i is a vowel.

Program -23] Display Absolute value of given number.

```
#include<stdio.h>
#include<conio.h>
#include<math.h>
main()
{
float number;
int res;
clrscr();
printf("Enter a number to calculate it's absolute value:");
scanf("%f",&number);
res = abs(number);
printf("Absolute value of %.2f = %d", number, res);
getch();
```

```
return 0;
}
```

Input:

Enter a number to calculate it's absolute value:23.56

Output:

Absolute value of 23.56 = 23

Program -24] Calculate value of Tan.

```
#include<stdio.h>
#include<conio.h>
#include<math.h>
main()
{
double res, a = 1;
clrscr();
res = tan(a);
printf("The tan(%lf) = %lf\n", a, res);
getch();
return 0;
}
```

Program -25] Print Round Up value of given number using Ceil function.

```
#include<stdio.h>
#include<conio.h>
#include<math.h>
void main()
{
double number, res;
clrscr();
printf("\nEnter a number to round it up:");
scanf("%lf",&number);
res = ceil(number);
printf("\nOriginal number = %lf\n", number);
printf("\nNumber rounded up = %lf\n", res);
getch();
}
```

Input:

Enter a number to round it up:56.75

Output:

Original number = 56.750000

Number rounded up = 57.000000

Program -26] Perform the use of atof()

This function of stdlib will convert a string to a double.

```
#include<stdio.h>
#include<conio.h>
#include<stdlib.h>
main()
{
char ac[20];
float res;
clrscr();
printf("Enter number in string format - ");
scanf("%s",&ac);
res = atof(ac);
printf("As a float number %4.2f\n",res);
getch();
return 0;
}
```

Program -27] Print the value of Cos.

```
#include<stdio.h>
#include<conio.h>
#include<math.h>
main()
{
double res, x = .25;
clrscr();
res = cos(x);
printf("The cos(%lf) = %lf\n", x, res);
getch();
return 0;
```

```
}
```

Output:

The cos(0.000000) = 1.000000

Program -28] Print current date & time.

```
#include <stdio.h>
#include <time.h>
#include <conio.h>
int main()
{
time_t t1;
char buffer[25];
struct tm* currenttm;
time(&t1);
currenttm = localtime(&t1);
strftime(buffer, 25, "%H:%M:%S:%d:%m:%Y", currenttm);
puts(buffer);
getch();
return 0;
}
```

Program -29] Program to display round down value of given no using floor function.

```
#include<stdio.h>
#include<conio.h>
#include<math.h>
void main()
{
double number, res;
clrscr();
printf("Enter a number :");
scanf("%lf",&number);
res = floor(number);
printf("\nOriginal number = %lf\n", number);
printf("\nNumber after rounded = %lf", res);
```

```
getch();
}
```

Input:

Enter a number : 54

Output:

Original number = 54.000000

Number after rounded = 54.000000

Program-30] Print Date & Time.

```
#include <stdio.h>
#include <stdlib.h>
#include <time.h>
int main()
{
time_t current;
time(&current);
printf("%s", ctime(&current));
getch();
return(0);
}
```

Program-31] Print log value of given no.

```
#include<stdio.h>
#include<conio.h>
#include<math.h>
void main()
{
double no, res;
clrscr();
printf("Enter a number for it’s natural log (base is e): ");
scanf("%lf",&no);
res = log(no);
printf("\nNatural log of %lf = %lf", no, res);
getch();
}
```

Input:

Enter a number for it's natural log (base is 10):4

Output:

Natural log of 4.0000 = 1.386294

Program -32] Find square root of given no.

```
#include<stdio.h>
#include<conio.h>
#include<math.h>
int main()
{
double no, res;
clrscr();
printf("\nEnter a number to calculate it's square root:");
scanf("%lf",&no);
res = sqrt(no);
printf("\nSquare root of %lf = %lf", no, res);
getch();
return(0);
}
```

Program -33] Calculate value of Log base 10.

```
#include<stdio.h>
#include<conio.h>
#include<math.h>
int main()
{
double no, res;
clrscr();
printf("Enter a number to calculate it's log (base is 10):");
scanf("%lf",&no);
res = log10(number);
printf("\nCommon log of %lf = %lf", no, res);
getch();
return(0);
}
```

Input:

Enter a number to calculate it's log (base is 10):90

Output:

Common log of 90.000000 = 1.954243

Program -34] Find sin Value.

```
#include<stdio.h>
#include<conio.h>
#include<math.h>
int main()
{
double result, a = 90;
clrscr();
res = sin(a);
printf("The sin(%lf) = %lf\n", a, res);
getch();
return(0);
}
```

Output:

The sin(90.0000) = 0.893997

Program -35] Find Power of value.

```
#include<stdio.h>
#include<conio.h>
#include<math.h>
int main()
{
double x, y, res;
clrscr();
printf("\nEnter x and y to calculate x^y:");
scanf("%lf%lf",&x, &y);
res = pow(x, y);
printf("\n%lf raised to %lf = %lf", x, y, res);
getch();
return(0);
}
```

Input:

Enter x and y to calculate x^y:2 3

Output:

2.00 raised to 3.00 = 8.00

Program -36] Calculate Power10 value of given no.

```
#include<stdio.h>
#include<conio.h>
#include<math.h>
int main()
{
int a = 5;
double res;
clrscr();
res = pow10(a);
printf("\nTen raised to %d is %lf\n", a, res);
getch();
return(0);
}
```

Output:

Ten raised to 5 is 100000.000000

Program -37] Program to rename file.

```
#include <conio.h>
#include <stdio.h>
int main()
{
clrscr();
//First argument source file and second rename file
rename("acme.txt", "it.txt");
printf("File renamed successfully...");
getch();
return(0);
}
```

Program -38] Program to change the textcolor of text.

```
#include<stdio.h>
#include<conio.h>
```

```
main()
{
clrscr();
textcolor(RED);
cprintf("C programming");
textcolor(GREEN);
cprintf(" Reference Boook");
getch();
return 0;
}
```

Program -39] Blinking Text.

```
#include<stdio.h>
#include<conio.h>
main()
{
clrscr();
textcolor(GREEN+BLINK);
cprintf("C programming ");
textcolor(RED+BLINK);
cprintf("Reference Book ");
textcolor(MAGENTA+BLINK);
cprintf(" By ACME IT Consultancy & Service");
getch();
return 0;
}
```

Program -40] Program to close in given time interval.

```
#include<stdio.h>
#include<conio.h>
#include<stdlib.h>
int main()
{
clrscr();
//Here 1000 interval = 1 second
printf("This c program will close in 5 seconds.\n");
```

```
delay(5000);
return 0;
}
```

Program -41] Program to change the cursor position.

```
#include<stdio.h>
#include<conio.h>
int main()
{
int a, b;
clrscr();
printf ("Enter value of x Axis");
scanf ("%d",&a);
printf ("Enter value of y Axis");
scanf ("%d",&b);
gotoxy(a,b);
printf("Current poision of cursor.");
getch();
return 0;
}
```

Program -42] Function wherey.

```
#include<stdio.h>
#include<conio.h>
int main()
{
int y;
clrscr();
printf("ACME\n");
y = wherey();
printf("Vertical cursor position the text appears = %d",y);
getch();
return 0;
}
```

Output:

```
ACME
```

Vertical cursor position the text appears = 2

Program -43] Function kbhit.

```
#include<stdio.h>
#include<conio.h>
main()
{
while(!kbhit())
printf("You haven't pressed a key.\n");
return 0;
}
```

Program -44] Program remove or delete file from bin directory.

```
#include <conio.h>
#include <stdio.h>
int main()
{
clrscr();
if (!remove("a.txt") )
{
printf("File removed successfully..\n");
}
else
{
printf("File not removed please check the file");
}
getch();
return(0);
}
```

Output: File removed successfully..

Program -45] Program to change the text background.

```
#include<stdio.h>
#include<conio.h>
int main()
```

```
{
clrscr();
textbackground(GREEN);
cprintf("C program to change background color.");
getch();
return 0;
}
```

Program -46] Program to display horizontal cursor position.

```
#include<stdio.h>
#include<conio.h>
main()
{
int x;
clrscr();
printf("ACME");
x = wherex();
printf("\nHorizontal cursor position the text appears = %d\n",x);
getch();
return 0;
}
```

Output:

```
ACME
Horizontal cursor position this text appears = 5
```

Program -47] Program to check alphanumeric characters.

```
#include<stdio.h>
#include<conio.h>
int main()
{
char x;
printf("Enter a character :");
scanf("%c",&x);
if(isalnum(x))
{
printf("It's alpha-numeric character \n");
```

```
}
else
{
printf("It's not alpha-numeric character");
}
getch();
return 0;
}
```

Input: Enter a character :a

Output: It'snot a alphanumeric character

Program -48] Program to check whether entered character is digit or not.

```
#include<stdio.h>
#include<conio.h>
int main()
{
char x;
printf("Enter a character :");
scanf("%c",&x);
if(isdigit(x))
{
printf("It's a digit\n");
}
else
{
printf("It's not a digit");
}
getch();
return 0;
}
```

Input: Enter a character :a

Output: It'snot a digit

Program -49] Calculate gross salary.

```
#include<stdio.h>
#include<conio.h>
```

```
void main()
{
float bp,da,hra,grpay;
clrscr();
printf("\nEnter the Basic Pay:");
scanf("%f",&bp);
da=0.4*bp;
hra=0.2*bp;
grpay=bp+da+hra;
printf("\nBasic Pay is=%f",bp);
printf("\nDearness Allowance is=%f",da);
printf("\nHouse Rent Allowance is=%f",hra);
printf("\nGross Pay is=%f",grpay);
getch();
}
```

Input:

Enter the Basic Pay:20000

Output:

Basic Pay is=20000.000000
Dearness Allowance is=8000.00
House Rent Allowance is=4000.00
Gross Pay is=32000.000000

Program -50] Calculate the sum of digits.

```
#include<stdio.h>
#include<conio.h>
void main()
{
int r,n,no;
int sum=0;
clrscr();
printf("\nEnter a 5 digit number in integer range:");
scanf("%d",&no);
r= no %10;
n= no /10;
sum=sum+r;
r=n%10;
```

```
n=n/10;
sum=sum+r;
r=n%10;
n=n/10;
sum=sum+r;
r=n%10;
sum=sum+r;
printf("\nThe sum of digits of %d is %d", no,sum);
getch();
}
```

Input:

Enter a 5 digit number:12345

Output:

The sum of the 5 digits of 12345 is 14

Program -51] Print reverse number using modulus operator.

```
#include<stdio.h>
#include<conio.h>
void main()
{
int x,n;
long int rev=0;
clrscr();
printf("\nEnter a 5 digit number: in integer range");
scanf("%d",&n);
x=n%10;
n=n/10;
rev=rev+x*10000L;
x=n%10;
n=n/10;
rev=rev+x*1000;
x=n%10;
n=n/10;
rev=rev+x*100;
x=n%10;
n=n/10;
rev=rev+x*10;
```

```
x=n%10;
rev=rev+x;
printf("\nThe reverse number is=%ld",rev);
getch();
}
```

Input:

Enter a 5 digit number:12345

Output:

The reverse number is=54321

Program -52] To calculate total number of illiterate Boys and Girls.

```
#include<stdio.h>
#include<conio.h>
main()
{
long int totpop=75000;
long int totboy,totlit,litboy,ilitboy,totgirl,totlitgirl,ilitgirl;
clrscr();
totboy=(48.0/100.0)*totpop;
printf("\nTotal no of boys in the town are:%ld",totboy);
totlit=(40.0/100.0)*totpop;
printf("\nTotal no of literate people are:%ld",totlit);
litboy=(30.0/100.0)*totpop;
printf("\nTotal no of literate boys are:%ld",litboy);
totlitgirl=totlit-litboy;
totgirl=totpop-totboy;
ilitboy=totboy-litboy;
ilitgirl=totgirl-totlitgirl;
printf("\nTotal no of Girls are:%ld",totgirl);
printf("\nTotal no of illiterate Boys are:%ld",ilitboy);
printf("\nTotal no of illiterate Girls are:%ld",ilitgirl);
getch();
return(0);
}
```

Output:

Total no of boys in the town are:35999

Total no of literate people are:30000

```
Total no of literate boys are:22499
Total no of girls are:39001
Total no of illiterate boys are:13500
Total no of illiterate girls are:31500
```

Program -53] Calculate Total No. Of Currency Notes Of Each Denomination.

```
#include<stdio.h>
#include<conio.h>
main()
{
int amt,hun,fifty,twenty,ten,five;
clrscr();
printf("\n Enter amount to withdrawn:");
scanf("%d",&amt);
hun=amt/100;
amt=amt%100;
fifty=amt/50;
amt=amt%50;
twenty=amt/20;
amt=amt%20;
ten=amt/10;
amt=amt%10;
five=amt/5;
amt=amt%5;
printf("\n No of Hundred Rs.notes =%d",hun);
printf("\n No of Fifty Rs.notes =%d",fifty);
printf("\n No of Twenty Rs.notes =%d",twenty);
printf("\n No of Ten Rs.notes =%d",ten);
printf("\n No of Five Rs.notes =%d",five);
getch();
return(0);
}
```

Input:

```
Enter amount to withdrawn:400
```

Output:

```
No of Hundred Rs.notes =4
```

No of Fifty Rs.notes =0
No of Twenty Rs.notes =0
No of Ten Rs.notes =0
No of Five Rs.notes =0

Program -54] Read & Write string.

```
#include<stdio.h>
#include<conio.h>
void main()
{
char sen[] = "ACMEIT";
clrscr();
printf("%s\n %6.4s",sen,sen);
getch();
}
```

Program -55] Calculate Square & Cube After & Previous No.

```
#include <stdio.h>
#include <conio.h>
int main()
{
int n,p,a;
clrscr();
printf ("Enter number");
scanf ("%d",&n);
printf("Square of number %d\n",n*n);
printf("Cube of number %d\n",n*n*n);
a=n+1;
printf("Square of next number %d\n",a*a);
printf("Cube of next number %d\n",a*a*a);
p=n-1;
printf("Square of previous number %d\n",p*p);
printf("Cube of previous number %d\n",p*p*p);
getch();
return(0);
}
```

Program -56]Program to fill entire screen with spade.

```
#include<stdio.h>
#include<conio.h>
void main()
{
char a;
int i,j;
a=6;
clrscr();
for(i=0;i<=26;i++)
{
for(j=0;j<=78;j++)
{
printf("%c",a);
}
printf("\n");
}
getch();
}
```

Program -57] Average of two float data type number's.

```
#include<stdio.h>
#include<conio.h>
main()
{
float a,b;
clrscr();
printf("Enter first number:");
scanf("%f",&a);
printf("Enter second number:");
scanf("%f",&b);
printf("Average of %2.f & %2f is=%2f",a,b,(a+b)/2);
getch();
return(0);
}
```

Input:
Enter first number:45
Enter second number:56
Output:
Average of 45 & 56.00 is=50.50

Program -58] Calculate Area of Circle using a math.h header file.

```
#include<stdio.h>
#include<conio.h>
#include<math.h>
main()
{
const float pi=3.14;
float r,ac;
clrscr();
printf("Enter radius of circle:");
scanf("%f",&r);
ac=pi*(pow(r,2));
printf("The area of circle is:%0.2f",ac);
getch();
return(0);
}
```

Input:
Enter radius of circle:2
Output:
The area of circle is:12.56

CHAPTER THREE

If Statement Programs

Program -59] Program to find whether given no is even or odd.

```
#include<stdio.h>
#include<conio.h>
main()
{
int n;
clrscr();
printf("\n Enter any no:");
scanf("%d",&n);
if(n%2==0)
printf("\n %d is Even no",n);
else
printf("%d is odd no",n);
getch();
return(0);
}
```

Input:

Enter any number:2

Output:

2 is Even number

Program -60] Find Maximum number between two number's.

```
#include<stdio.h>
#include<conio.h>
main()
{
int no1=56,no2=89;
```

```
clrscr();
if(no1>no2)
printf("\n The First Number %d is Maximum.",no1);
else
printf("\n The Second Number %d is Maximum.",no2);
getch();
return(0);
}
```

Output:

The Second Number 89 is Maximum.

Program -61] Find Maximum Number between three number's.

```
#include<stdio.h>
#include<conio.h>
main()
{
int no1,no2,no3;
clrscr();
printf("Enter first number :");
scanf("%d",&no1);
printf("Enter second number:");
scanf("%d",&no2);
printf("Enter third number :");
scanf("%d",&no3);
if(no1>no2 && no1>no3)
printf("\n The First Number %d is Maximum.",no1);
else if(no2>no1 && no2>no3)
printf("\n The Second Number %d is Maximum.",no2);
else
printf("\n The Third Number %d is Maximum.",no3);
getch();
return(0);
}
```

Input:

Enter first number :5

Enter second number:2

Enter third number :5

Output:
The Third Number 5 is Maximum.

Program -62] Find Minimum Number between two number's.

```
#include<stdio.h>
#include<conio.h>
#include<math.h>
main()
{
int no1,no2;
clrscr();
printf("Enter the first number :");
scanf("%d",&no1);
printf("Enter the second number:");
scanf("%d",&no2);
if(no1<no2)
printf("\n The First Number %d is Minimum.",no1);
else
printf("\n The Second Number %d is Minimum.",no2);
getch();
return(0);
}
```

Input:
Enter the first number :5
Enter the second number:6
Output:
The First Number 5 is Minimum.

Program -63] Find Minimum Number between three number's.

```
#include<stdio.h>
#include<conio.h>
main()
{
int no1,no2,no3;
clrscr();
printf("Enter first number :");
```

```
scanf("%d",&no1);
printf("Enter second number:");
scanf("%d",&no2);
printf("Enter third number :");
scanf("%d",&no3);
if(no1<no2 && no1<no3)
printf("\n The First Number %d is Minimum.",no1);
else if(no2<no1 && no2<no3)
printf("\n The Second Number %d is Minimum.",no2);
else
printf("\n The Third Number %d is Minimum.",no3);
getch();
return(0);
}
```

Input:

Enter first number :5
Enter second number:6
Enter third number :2

Output:

The Third Number 2 is Minimum.

Program -64] Check Whether given year is leap or not.

```
#include<stdio.h>
#include<conio.h>
void main()
{
int year;
clrscr();
printf("Enter a year to check if it is a leap year:");
scanf("%d", &year);
if ( year%400 == 0)
printf("%d is a leap year.\n", year);
else if ( year%100 == 0)
printf("%d is not a leap year.\n", year);
else if ( year%4 == 0 )
printf("%d is a leap year.\n", year);
else
```

```
printf("%d is not a leap year.\n", year);
getch();
}
```

Input:

Enter a year to check if it is a leap year:1012

Output:

1012 is a leap year.

Program -65] Program calculate Profit & Loss per Item.

```
#include<stdio.h>
#include<conio.h>
main()
{
float purpri,sellpri,profit,loss;
clrscr();
printf("\nEnter cost price:");
scanf("%f",& purpri);
printf("\nEnter selling price:");
scanf("%f",& sellpri);
profit = sellpri - purpri;
loss = purpri - sellpri;
if(profit >0)
printf("\n Seller has made Profit of Rs.%f", profit);
if(loss >0)
printf("\n Seller is in loss by Rs.%f", loss);
if(profit ==0)
printf("\n No Profit and No Loss");
getch();
return(0);
}
```

Input:

Enter cost price:2000

Enter selling price:2050

Output:

Seller has made Profit of Rs.50.00

Program -66] Program to determine whether the point lies within the circle or not.

```
#include<stdio.h>
#include<conio.h>
void main()
{
int a,b,r;
int c,d;
clrscr();
printf("\n Enter radius of circle and co-ordinate of the point:");
scanf("%d%d%d",&r,&a,&b);
d=a*a+b*b;
c=r*r;
if(d==c)
printf("\nGiven Point is on the circle");
else
{
if(d>c)
printf("\nGiven Point is outside the circle");
else
printf("\nGiven Point is inside the circle");
}
getch();
}
```

Input:

Enter the radius of circle and coordinate of the point:

Radius:2

x:1

y:2

Output:

Point is outside the circle

Program -67] Find out the day of 1st January.

```
#include<stdio.h>
#include<conio.h>
void main()
{
```

```
int ldays,fday,year,tyear;
long int ndays,tdays;
clrscr();
printf("\n Enter the year:");
scanf("%d",&year);
tyear = year;
ndays=(year-1)*365L;
ldays=(year-1)/4-(year-1)/100+(year-1)/400;
tdays=ndays+ldays;
fday=tdays%7;
printf("\n First Day of year %d is",tyear);
if(fday==0)
printf(" Monday");
if(fday==1)
printf(" Tuesday");
if(fday==2)
printf(" Wednesday");
if(fday==3)
printf(" Thursday");
if(fday==4)
printf(" Friday");
if(fday==5)
printf(" Saturday");
if(fday==6)
printf(" Sunday");
getch();
}
```

Input:

Enter the year:2012

Output:

First Day of year 2012 is Sunday

Program -68] Find out triangle is valid or not.

```
#include<stdio.h>
#include<conio.h>
void main()
{
```

```
float first,second,third;
clrscr();
printf("\nEnter 3 angles of triangle:");
scanf("%f%f%f", &first,&second,&third);
if((first+second+third)==180)
printf("\nTriangle is a valid...");
else
printf("\nTriangle is invalid...");
getch();
}
```

Input:

Enter 3 angles of triangle:
60
60
60

Output:

Triangle is a valid...

Program -69] Find Out Point Lies On X-Axis , Y-Axis Or On The Origin.

```
#include<stdio.h>
#include<conio.h>
void main()
{
int a,b;
clrscr();
printf("\n Enter the x and y coordinates of point:");
scanf("%d%d",&a,&b);
if(a==0 && b==0)
printf("\n Entered point is an origin");
else
if(a==0 &&b!=0)
printf("\n Entered point lies on Y axis");
else
if(a!=0 && b==0)
printf("\n Entered point lies on X axis");
else
printf("\n Entered point not on any axis, nor origin");
```

```
getch();
}
```

Input:

Enter the x and y coordinates of point

x:0

y:1

Output:

Point lies on Y axis

Program -70] Find out Absolute value of number without function.

```
#include<stdio.h>
#include<conio.h>
void main()
{
int n;
clrscr();
printf("\n Enter number :");
scanf("%d",&n);
if(n<0)
{
n=n*-1;
}
printf("\n Absolute value is %d",n);
getch();
}
```

Input:

Enter number 56.23

Output:

Absolute value is 56

Program -71] Program to check whether points are Collinear or not.

```
#include<stdio.h>
#include<conio.h>
#include<math.h>
void main()
{
```

```
int a1,a2,a3,b1,b2,b3;
int l1,l2,l3;
clrscr();
printf("\n Enter x1 and y1 co-ordinates for first point:");
scanf("%d%d",&a1,&b1);
printf("\n Enter x2 and y2 co-ordinates for second point:");
scanf("%d%d",&a2,&b2);
printf("\n Enter x3 and y3 coordinates for third point:");
scanf("%d%d",&a3,&b3);
l1=(float)abs(a2-a1)/abs(b2-b1);
l2=(float)abs(a3-a1)/abs(b3-b1);
l3=(float)abs(a3-a2)/abs(b3-b2);
if((l1==l2)&&(l1==l3))
printf("\n Given points are collinear");
else
printf("\n Given points are not collinear");
getch();
}
```

Input:

Enter x1 and y1 co-ordinates for first point:

x1:1

y1:2

Enter x2 and y2 co-ordinates for second point:

x2:2

y2:3

Enter x3 and y3 co-ordinates for third point:

x3:4

y3:5

Output:

Given Points are collinear

Program -72] To Check Type Of Character entered by user.

```
#include<stdio.h>
#include<conio.h>
void main()
{
char ch;
```

```
clrscr();
printf("\n Enter a character from keyboard:");
scanf("%c",&ch);
if(ch>=65 && ch<=90)
printf("\n The character is an uppercase letter");
if(ch>=97 && ch<=122)
printf("\n The character is an lowercase letter");
if(ch>=48 && ch<=57)
printf("\n The character is digit");
if((ch>=0 && ch<48)||(ch>57 && ch<65)||(ch>90 && ch<97) || ch>122)
printf("\n The character is special symbol");
getch();
}
```

Input:

Enter a character from keyboard:A

Output:

The character is an uppercase letter

Program -73] Program to calculate fine for late return of book.

```
#include<stdio.h>
#include<conio.h>
void main()
{
int days;
float fine;
clrscr();
printf("\n Enter no. of due days:");
scanf("%d",&days);
if(days>=1 && days<=10)
{
fine = days* 0.50;
printf("\n Fine=Rs.%0.2f",fine);
}
else
{
if (days>=10 && days<=20)
{
```

```
printf("\n Fine=Rs.%d",days*1);
}
else
{
if(days>=20 && days<=30)
{
printf("\n Fine=Rs.%d",days*5);
}
else
{
printf("\n The membership has been cancelled");
}
}
}
getch();
}
```

Input:

Enter no due days :20

Output:

Fine=Rs.100

Program -74] Program to check whether triangle is valid or not by given side.

```
#include<stdio.h>
#include<conio.h>
void main()
{
int s1,s2,s3,p,sum;
clrscr();
printf("\n Enter three sides of triangle:");
scanf("%d%d%d",&s1,&s2,&s3);
if(s1>s2)
{
if(s1>s3)
{
sum=s2+s3;
p=s1;
```

```
}
else
{
sum=s1+s2;
p=s3;
}
}
else
{
if(s2>s3)
{
sum=s1+s3;
p=s2;
}
else
{
sum=s1+s2;
p=s3;
}
}
if(sum>p)
printf("\n The triangle is valid");
else
printf("\n The triangle is invalid");
getch();
}
```

Input:

Enter three sides of triangle:
Side1:4
Side2:4
Side3:4

Output:

The triangle is valid

Program -75] Program to check the type of triangle.

```
#include<stdio.h>
#include<conio.h>
```

```
void main()
{
int side1, side2, side3,a,b,c;
clrscr();
printf("\n Enter three sides of triangle:");
scanf("%d%d%d", & side1,& side2,& side3 );
a=( side1* side1)==( side2* side2)+( side3* side3);
b=( side2* side2)==( side1* side1)+( side3* side3);
c=( side3* side3)==( side1* side1)+( side2* side2);
if(side1!= side2 && side2!= side3 && side3!= side1)
printf("\n Triangle is a scalene triangle");
if((side1== side2) &&( side2!= side3))
printf("\n Triangle is an issosceles triangle");
if((side2== side3) &&( side3!= side1))
printf("\n Triangle is an issosceles triangle");
if((side1== side3) &&( side3!= side2))
printf("\n Triangle is an issosceles triangle");
if((side1== side2) &&( side2== side3))
printf("\n Triangle is an equilateral triangle");
if(a||b||c)
printf("\n Triangle is right angled triangle");
getch();
}
```

Input:

Enter three sides of triangle:

Side1:4

Side2:4

Side3:4

Output:

Triangle is an equilateral triangle

Program -76] Program to find out odd & even number usign goto statement

```
#include<stdio.h>
#include<conio.h>
#include<stdlib.h>
int main()
```

```
{
int a;
char sel;
clrscr();
start:
printf("\n Enter number to check even or odd:");
scanf("%d",&a);
if(a%2==0)
printf("\nThe entered number %d is Even.", a);
else
printf("\nThe entered number %d is Odd.", a);
printf("\nEnter number again. to continue press y (y/n):");
scanf("%s",& sel);
if((sel=='Y')||( sel =='y'))
goto start;
if((sel =='N')||( sel =='n'))
exit(0);
getch();
return(0);
}
```

Input:

Enter number to check even or odd:2

Output:

The entered number 2 is Even.

Input:

Enter number again. to continue press y (y/n):y

Enter number:3

Output:

The entered number 3 is Odd.

Input:

Enter number again. to continue press y (y/n)::n

Program -77] Program to perform multiplication operation without (*).

usign goto statement

```
#include<stdio.h>
#include<conio.h>
#include<stdlib.h>
```

```
int main()
{
int i,a,b,prod=0;
clrscr();
printf("\n Enter First number:");
scanf("%d",&a);
printf("\n Enter Second number:");
scanf("%d",&b);
for (i=1;i<=b;i++)
{
prod = prod + a;
}
printf ("Multiplication of two numbers %d ",prod);
getch();
return(0);
}
```

Input:

Enter the First number:5

Enter the Second number:6

Output:

Multiplication of two numbers 30

CHAPTER FOUR

Conditional Operator Programs

Program -78] Program to check whether the character entered through the

keyboard is a lowercase or not using conditional operator.

```
#include<stdio.h>
#include<conio.h>
void main()
{
char ch;
clrscr();
printf("\nEnter character:");
scanf("%c",&ch);
ch>=97 && ch<=122?printf("\n character entered is in
lowercase"):printf("\n character entered is not in lowercase");
getch();
}
```

Input:

Enter character:a

Output:

Character entered is in lowercase

Program -79] Program using conditional operator to determine whether a year

enterd through the ketboard is leap year or not.

```
#include<stdio.h>
#include<conio.h>
```

```
void main()
{
int yr;
clrscr();
printf("\nEnter year:");
scanf("%d",&yr);
yr%100==0?(yr%400==0?printf("\nIs Leap year"):printf("\n Is not leap
yr")):(yr%4==0?
printf("Is Leap year"):printf("Is not a leap year"));
getch();
}
```

Input:
Enter year:2012
Output:
Is Leap year

Program -80] To find greatest number using conditional operator.

```
#include<stdio.h>
#include<conio.h>
void main()
{
int n1,n2,n3,max;
clrscr();
printf("\nEnter three numbers:");
scanf("%d%d%d",&n1,&n2,&n3);
max=n1>n2?(n1>n3?n1:n3):(n2>n3?n2:n3);
printf("\nMaximum number is %d",max);
getch();
}
```

Input:
Enter three numbers:
Number1:5
Number2:6
Number3:4
Output:
Maximum number is 6

CHAPTER FIVE

While Loop Programs

Program -81] Program to print infinite loop.

```
#include<stdio.h>
#include<conio.h>
void main()
{
int i=1;
clrscr();
while(i!=0)
{
printf("\n%d",i);
i++;
}
getch();
}
```

Program -82] Program to print the sum of digits of a given number.

```
#include<stdio.h>
#include<conio.h>
void main()
{
int n,r,sum=0;
clrscr();
printf("\nEnter any no:");
scanf("%d",&n);
while(n>0)
{
r = n%10;
```

```
sum = sum+r;
n=n/10;
}
printf("Sum of digits is %d\n",sum);
getch();
}
```

Input:

Enter any no:123

Ouput:

Sum of digits is 6

Program -83] Program to print the product of digits of a given numbers.

```
#include<stdio.h>
#include<conio.h>
void main()
{
int n,r,product=1;
clrscr();
printf("\n Enter any no:");
scanf("%d",&n);
while(n>0)
{
r = n%10;
product = product * r;
n=n/10;
}
printf("Product of digits is: %d\n",product);
getch();
}
```

Input:

Enter any no:23

Output:

Product of digits is: 6

Program -84] Program to check whether the given no is magic or not .

```
#include<stdio.h>
```

```
#include<conio.h>
main()
{
int n,r,sum=0,no;
clrscr();
printf("\nEnter any no:");
scanf("%d",&n);
no=n;
while(n>0)
{
r=n%10;
sum = sum + r * r * r;
n = n / 10;
}
if(sum==no)
printf("%d is magic no\n",no);
else
printf("%d is not magic no\n",no);
getch();
return(0);
}
```

Input:

Enter any no:371

Output:

371 is magic no

Program -85] Print reverse number of given number.

```
#include<stdio.h>
#include<conio.h>
void main()
{
int n,r,rev=0;
clrscr();
printf("\nEnter any number:");
scanf("%d",&n);
while(n>0)
{
```

```
r = n % 10;
rev = rev * 10 +r;
n = n/10;
}
printf("Reverse no. is %d ",rev);
getch();
}
```

Input:

Enter any number: 1221

Output:

Reverse no. is 1221

Program -86] Program to check whether the given no is palindrome or not.

```
#include<stdio.h>
#include<conio.h>
void main()
{
int n,no,r,rev=0;
clrscr();
printf("\nEnter any number:");
scanf("%d",&n);
no=n;
while(n>0)
{
r = n % 10;
rev = rev * 10 +r;
n = n/10;
}
if(rev==no)
printf("%d is palindrome",no);
else
printf("%d is not palindrome",no);
getch();
}
```

Input:

Enter any number:121

Output:
121 is palindrome

Program -87] Print all the ASCII values and their equivalent characters using while loop .

```
#include<stdio.h>
#include<conio.h>
void main()
{
int j=0;
clrscr();
while(j<=255)
{
printf("%d%c\t",j,j);
j++;
}
printf("\n Press any key to exit...");
getch();
}
```

Program -88] Program to print next prime palindrome number.

```
#include<stdio.h>
#include<math.h>
#define TRUE 1
void main()
{
long n, t, b = 0, c, d;
printf("Enter an integer:");
scanf("%ld",&n); /* n must be a natural number */
while(TRUE)
{
n++;
t=n;
while(t)
{
b*=10;
```

```
b+=t%10;
t/=10;
}
if(b==n)
{
d=(int)sqrt(n);
for(c=2; c<=d; c++)
{
if(n%c==0)
break;
}
if(c==d+1)
break;
}
b=0;
}
printf("%ld\n",n);
getch();
}
```

Input:

Enter an integer:371

Output:

373

Program -89] Program to calculate overtime pay of employees.

```
#include<stdio.h>
#include<conio.h>
void main()
{
float opay;
int hr,i=1,n;
clrscr();
printf("\nEnter how many employee:");
scanf("%d",&n);
while(i<=n)
{
printf("\nEnter no of hours worked:");
```

```
scanf("%d",&hr);
if(hr>=45)
{
opay=(hr-45)*12;
printf("\nNo of hours worked is %d\nOvertime pay=Rs.%f",hr,opay);
}
else
{
opay=0;
printf("\nNo of hours worked %d is less than 40 hrs.\nHence no overtime pay",hr);
}
i++;
}
getch();
}
```

Input:

Enter how many employee:2

1 Employee

Enter no of hours worked:46

Output:

No of hours worked is 46

Overtime pay=Rs.12.000000

Input:

2 Employee

Enter no of hours worked:47

Output:

No of hours worked is 47

Overtime pay=Rs.24.000000

Program -90] Program to decide whether a number is positive,negative or zero.

```
#include<stdio.h>
#include<conio.h>
void main()
{
int p,n,z,no;
```

```
char choice='y';
clrscr();
p=0;
n=0;
z=0;
while(choice=='y'||choice=='Y')
{
printf("\nEnter a number:");
scanf("%d",&no);
if(no==0)
z++;
if(no>0)
p++;
if(no<0)
n++;
fflush(stdin);
printf("Do you want to continue (y/n):?");
scanf("%c",&choice);
}
printf("\nYou entered %d positive numbers",p);
printf("\nYou entered %d negative numbers",n);
printf("\nYou entered %d zeros",z);
getch();
}
```

Input:

Enter a number:2

Do you want to continue (y/n):?y

Enter a number:3

Do you want to continue (y/n):?y

Enter a number:-9

Do you want to continue (y/n):?y

Enter a number:-6

Do you want to continue (y/n):?y

Enter a number:0

Do you want to continue (y/n):?y

Enter a number:0

Do you want to continue (y/n):?n

Output:

You entered 2 positive numbers
You entered 2 negative numbers
You entered 2 zeros

Program -91] Program to reverse a no and find octal equivalent of reversed no.

```
#include<stdio.h>
#include<conio.h>
#include<math.h>
void main()
{
int x,no1,no2,r,octal;
clrscr();
printf("\nEnter any no:");
scanf("%d",&no1);
no2=0;
while(no1>0)
{
r=no1%10;
no2=no2*10+r;
no1=no1/10;
}
no1=no2;
x=octal=0;
while(no1>0)
{
r=no1%8;
no1=no1/8;
octal=octal+r*pow(10,x);
x++;
}
printf("\nThe octal equivalent of %d is %d",no2,octal);
getch();
}
```

Input:
Enter any no:112
Output:

The octal equivalent of 211 is 323

CHAPTER SIX

For Loop Programs

Program -92] Program to find X raise to Y.

```
#include<stdio.h>
#include<conio.h>
void main()
{
int a,n,i,prod=1;
clrscr();
printf("\nEnter Base:");
scanf("%d",&a);
printf("\nEnter power:");
scanf("%d",&n);
for(i=1;i<=n;i++)
prod=prod*a;
printf("\n%d is raised to %d is %d\n",a,n,prod);
getch();
}
```

Input:

Enter Base:5

Enter power:3

Output:

5 is raised to 3 is 125

Program -93] Program to print the Series from 1 to 10.

```
#include<stdio.h>
#include<conio.h>
main()
{
```

```
int i;
clrscr();
printf("The series is:\n");
for(i=1;i<=10;i++)
{
printf("%d\n",i);
}
getch();
return(0);
}
```

Output:

```
The series is:
1
2
3
4
5
6
7
8
9
10
```

Program -94] Program to print the table of a given number.

```
#include<stdio.h>
#include<conio.h>
main()
{
int no,i,table=0;
clrscr();
printf("Enter the number:");
scanf("%d",&no);
printf("\nThe Table of %d is\n",no);
for(i=1;i<=10;i++)
{
table=no*i;
printf("%d\n",table);
```

```
}
getch();
return(0);
}
```

Input:

Enter the number:29

Output:

The Table of 29 is
29
58
87
116
145
174
203
232
261
290

Program -95] Program to print the nth Fibbonacci series.

```
#include<stdio.h>
#include<conio.h>
main()
{
int n,f=0,f1=1,f2=1,i;
clrscr();
printf("\nEnter order of series:");
scanf("%d",&n);
printf("%4d\n",f1);
printf("%4d\n",f2);
for(i=3;i<n;i++)
{
f=f1+f2;
printf("%4d\n",f);
f1=f2;
f2=f;
}
```

```
getch();
return(0);
}
```

Input

Enter order of series:10

Output:

1
1
2
3
5
8
13
21
34

Program -96] Find Maximum Number from 10 no's.

```
#include<stdio.h>
#include<conio.h>
main()
{
int no,i,max=0;
clrscr();
printf("Enter the 10 element:");
for(i=0;i<10;i++)
{
scanf("%d",&no);
if(no>max)
max=no;
}
printf("\nThe Number %d is Maximum.",max);
getch();
return(0);
}
```

Input:

Enter the 10 element:22 56 89 78 45 12 63 52 59 23

Output:

The Number 89 is Maximum.

Program -97] Find Minimum number from 10 no's.

```
#include<stdio.h>
#include<conio.h>
main()
{
int no,i,min;
clrscr();
printf("Enter the 10 elements:");
for(i=0;i<10;i++)
{
scanf("%d",&no);
if(no<min)
min=no;
}
printf("\nThe Number %d is Minimum.",min);
getch();
return(0);
}
```

Input:

Enter the 10 elements:22 56 89 78 45 12 63 52 59 23

Output:

The Number 12 is Minimum.

Program -98] Program to find Magic no from 1 to 1000 nos.

```
#include<stdio.h>
#include<conio.h>
main()
{
int n,no,r,sum=0;
clrscr();
for(n=1;n<=1000;n++)
{
no=n;
while(no>0)
```

```
{
r = no % 10;
sum = sum + r * r *r;
no = no / 10;
}
if(sum==n)
printf("%d\n",n);
sum=0;
}
getch();
return(0);
}
```

Output:

The Magic Numbers are:
1
153
370
371
407

Program -99] Program to find the palindrome nos. between 1 to 200.

```
#include<stdio.h>
#include<conio.h>
main()
{
int n,no,r,rev=0;
clrscr();
for(n=1;n<=200;n++)
{
no=n;
while(no>0)
{
r = no % 10;
rev = r + (rev * 10);
no = no/10;
}
if(rev==n)
```

```
printf("%5d",n);
rev=0;
}
getch();
return(0);
}
```

Output:

The Palindrom numbers are:

1 2 3 4 5 6 7 8 9 11 22 33 44 55 66 77
88 99 101 111 121 131 141 151 161 171 181 191

Program -100] Program to check whether given no is prime or not.

```
#include<stdio.h>
#include<conio.h>
main()
{
int n,i,pr=1;
clrscr();
printf("Enter the number:");
scanf("%d",&n);
for(i=2;i<n;i++)
{
if(n%i==0)
{
pr=0;
break;
}
}
if(pr==1)
printf("%d is prime",n);
else
printf("%d is not prime",n);
getch();
return(0);
}
```

Input:

Enter the number:7

Output:
7 is prime

Program -101] Print Prime number from 1 To 100.

```
#include<stdio.h>
#include<conio.h>
void main()
{
int n,j,k,fact=0;
clrscr();
for(j=0;j<100;j++)
{
fact=0;
for(k=1;k<=j;k++)
{
if(j%k==0)
fact++;
}
if(fact==2)
printf("\t%d",j);
}
getch();
}
```

Output:
The Prime numbers are:
2 3 5 7 11 13 17 19 23
29 31 37 41 43 47 53 59 61 67
71 73 79 83 89 97

Program -102] Program to check whether given no is perfect or not.

```
#include<stdio.h>
#include<conio.h>
main()
{
int n,no,i,fact=0;
clrscr();
```

```
printf("\nEnter any number:");
scanf("%d",&n);
no=n;
for(i=1;i<=n-1;i++)
{
if(n%i==0)
fact = fact+i;
}
if(fact==no)
printf("%d is perfect no",n);
else
printf("%d is not perfect no",n);
getch();
return(0);
}
```

Input:

Enter any number:6

Output:

6 is perfect no

Program -103] Program to print perfect nos between 1 to 1000.

```
#include<stdio.h>
#include<conio.h>
main()
{
int no,n,fact=0,i,j;
clrscr();
printf("\n Perfect nos between 1 to 1000 are:\n");
for(j=1;j<=1000;j++)
{
fact=0;
no=j;
for(i=1;i<=(j-1);i++)
{
if(j%i==0)
fact = fact+i;
}
```

```
if(fact==j)
printf("%4d",no);
}
getch();
return(0);
}
```

Output:

Perfect nos between 1 to 1000 are:
6 28 496

Program -104] Program to print all triplets(a,b,c) such that a2+b2=c2 where each a,b,c is between 1 and 100.

```
#include<stdio.h>
#include<conio.h>
main()
{
int i=1,j,k,a,b,c;
clrscr();
for(i=1;i<=50;i++)
{
for(j=1;j<=50;j++)
{
for(k=1;k<=50;k++)
{
a = i*i;
b = j*j;
c= k*k;
if(c==(a+b))
printf("\n a=%d b=%d c=%d",i,j,k);
}
}
}
getch();
return(0);
}
```

Output:

a=3 b=4 c=5
a=4 b=3 c=5
a=6 b=8 c=10
a=8 b=6 c=10

Program -105] Program to find the factorial of given no.

```
#include<stdio.h>
#include<conio.h>
main()
{
int n,i,fact=1;
clrscr();
printf("Enter no:");
scanf("%d",&n);
for(i=1;i<=n;i++)
fact=fact*i;
printf("\nFactorial of %d is %d\n",n,fact);
getch();
return(0);
}
```

Input:

Enter no:5

Output:

Factorial of 5 is 120

Program-106] Addition of N numbers.

```
#include<stdio.h>
#include<conio.h>
main()
{
int n, sum = 0, c, var;
clrscr();
printf("Enter the number of integers you want to add:");
scanf("%d",&n);
printf("Enter %d numbers\n",n);
for ( c = 1 ; c <= n ; c++ )
```

```
{
scanf("%d",&var);
sum = sum + var;
}
printf("\nSum of entered numbers = %d\n",sum);
getch();
return 0;
}
```

Input:

Enter the number of integers you want to add:3
Enter 3 numbers
4
5
6

Output:

Sum of entered numbers = 15

Program -107] Program to print N Random numbers.

```
#include<stdio.h>
#include<conio.h>
#include<stdlib.h>
void main()
{
int n, max, num, c;
clrscr();
printf("Enter the number of random numbers you want:");
scanf("%d",&n);
printf("Enter the maximum value of random number:");
scanf("%d",&max);
printf("\n%d random numbers from 0 to %d are :-\n",n,max);
randomize();
for (c=1;c<=n;c++)
{
num=random(max);
printf("%d\n",num);
}
getch();
```

```
}
```

Input:

Enter the number of random numbers you want:3

Enter the maximum value of random number:5

Output:

3 random numbers from 0 to 5 are :-

0

0

1

Program -108] Program to perform delay operation.

```
#include<conio.h>
#include<stdio.h>
void main()
{
int c,d;
clrscr();
for ( c=1;c<=3276;c++)
for (d=1;d<=3276;d++)
{
}
getch();
}
```

Program -109]Program to fill entire screen with smiling face.

```
#include<stdio.h>
#include<conio.h>
void main()
{
char a;
int i,j;
a=1;
clrscr();
for(i=0;i<=26;i++)
{
for(j=0;j<=78;j++)
```

```
{
printf("%c",a);
}
printf("\n");
}
getch();
}
```

Program -110] Program to generate all posssible combinations of 1,2,3 .

```
#include<stdio.h>
#include<conio.h>
void main()
{
int p=1,q=1,r=1;
clrscr();
for(p=1;p<=3;p++)
{
for(q=1;q<=3;q++)
{
for(r=1;r<=3;r++)
printf("%d%d%d\t",p,q,r);
}
}
getch();
}
```

Output:

```
111 112 113 121 122 123 131 132 133 211
212 213 221 222 223 231 232 233 311 312
313 321 322 323 331 332 333
```

Program -111] Program to produce intelligence table .

```
#include<stdio.h>
#include<conio.h>
void main()
{
int q,num=0;
```

```
float j,p;
clrscr();
for(q=1;q<=9;q++)
{
for(p=7.5;p<=15.5;p+=0.5)
{
j=2+(q+0.5*p);
printf("\nq=%d,p=%f,j=%f",q,p,j);
num++;
if(num>=20)
{
printf("\nPress any key to continue...");
getch();
num=0;
clrscr();
}
}
}
getch();
}
```

Program -112] Program to calculate the compound interest.

```
#include<stdio.h>
#include<conio.h>
main()
{
float priamt,q,r,n,amt;
int i;
for(i=0;i<1;i++)
{
clrscr();
printf("\nEnter the principle amount:");
scanf("%f",& priamt);
printf("\nEnter the rate of interest:");
scanf("%f",&r);
printf("\nEnter the no of years:");
scanf("%f",&n);
```

```
printf("\nEnter the compounding period:");
scanf("%f",&q);
amt = priamt +pow((1+(r/q)),(n/q));
printf("\nTotal amount=%f", amt);
}
getch();
return(0);
}
```

Input:

Enter the principle amount:20000
Enter the rate of interest:7
Enter the no of years:1
Enter the compounding period:1

Output:

Total amount=20255.000000

CHAPTER SEVEN

Pattern Programs

Program -113] Print Pattern - 1

```
*
***
*****
***
*
```

```
#include<stdio.h>
#include<conio.h>
main()
{
int n, c, k, space = 1;
clrscr();
printf("Enter number of rows:");
scanf("%d",&n);
space = n - 1;
for ( k = 1 ; k <= n ; k++ )
{
for ( c = 1 ; c <= space ; c++ )
printf(" ");
space--;
for ( c = 1 ; c <= 2*k-1 ; c++)
printf("*");
printf("\n");
}
space = 1;
for ( k = 1 ; k <= n - 1 ; k++ )
{
for ( c = 1 ; c <= space; c++)
```

```
printf(" ");
space++;
for ( c = 1 ; c <= 2*(n-k)-1 ; c++ )
printf("*");
printf("\n");
}
getch();
return 0;
}
```

Program -114] Program to print the following output.

```
*
* * *
* * * * *
* * * * * *
#include<stdio.h>
#include<conio.h>
main()
{
int row, c, n, temp;
clrscr();
printf("Enter the number of rows in pyramid of stars you wish to see: ");
scanf("%d",&n);
temp = n;
for ( row = 1 ; row <= n ; row++ )
{
for ( c = 1 ; c < temp ; c++ )
printf(" ");
temp--;
for ( c = 1 ; c <= 2*row - 1 ; c++ )
printf("*");
printf("\n");
}
getch();
return 0;
}
```

Program -115] Program to print following output.

```
*
* *
* * *
* * * *
* * * * *
#include<stdio.h>
#include<conio.h>
main()
{
int i,j;
clrscr();
for(i=1;i<=5;i++)
{
for(j=1;j<=i;j++)
printf("*");
printf("\n");
}
getch();
return(0);
}
```

Program -116] To Print Pattern.

```
12345
1234
123
12
1
#include<stdio.h>
#include<conio.h>
main()
{
int n, c, k, space;
clrscr();
printf("Enter a level:");
scanf("%d", &n);
```

```
space = 0;
for ( k = n ; k >= 1 ; k-- )
{
for ( c = 1 ; c <= space ; c++ )
printf(" ");
space++;
for ( c = 1 ; c <= k ; c++)
printf("%d", c);
printf("\n");
}
getch();
return 0;
}
```

Program -117] To Print Pattern.

```
A B C D E F G H
A B C D E F G
A B C D E F
A B C D E
A B C D
A B C
A B
A
#include<stdio.h>
#include<conio.h>
main()
{
char ch = 'A';
int n, c, k, space = 0;
clrscr();
printf("Enter the level:");
scanf("%d", &n);
for ( k = n ; k >= 1 ; k-- )
{
for ( c = 1 ; c <= space ; c++)
printf(" ");
space++;
```

```
for ( c = 1 ; c <= k ; c++ )
{
printf("%c ", ch);
ch++;
}
printf("\n");
ch = 'A';
}
getch();
return 0;
}
```

Program -118] To Print Pattern.

```
1
10
1010
10101
#include<stdio.h>
#include<conio.h>
main()
{
int n, c, k, num = 1;
clrscr();
printf("Enter the level:");
scanf("%d", &n);
for ( c = 1 ; c <= n ; c++ )
{
for ( k = 1 ; k <= c ; k++ )
{
printf("%d", num);
if ( num == 0 )
num = 1;
else
num = 0;
}
printf("\n");
}
```

```
getch();
return 0;
}
```

Program -119] To Print Pattern.

```
p
pr
pro
prog
progr
progra
program
#include<stdio.h>
#include<conio.h>
#include<string.h>
main()
{
char string[100];
int c, k, length;
clrscr();
printf("Enter a string:");
gets(string);
length = strlen(string);
for ( c = 0 ; c < length ; c++ )
{
for( k = 0 ; k <= c ; k++ )
{
printf("%c", string[k]);
}
printf("\n");
}
getch();
return 0;
}
```

Program -120] To Print Pattern.

```
1
121
12321
1234321
123454321
#include<stdio.h>
#include<conio.h>
main()
{
int n, c, k, x = 1;
clrscr();
printf("Enter the level:");
scanf("%d", &n);
for ( c = 1 ; c <= n ; c++ )
{
for ( k = 1 ; k <= c ; k++ )
{
printf("%d", x);
x++;
}
x--;
for ( k = 1 ; k <= c - 1 ; k++ )
{
x--;
printf("%d", x);
}
printf("\n");
x = 1;
}
getch();
return 0;
}
```

Program -121] To Print Pattern.

```
1 1
12 21
12321
```

```
#include<stdio.h>
#include<conio.h>
main()
{
int n, k, c, space, x, num = 1;
clrscr();
printf("Enter the level:");
scanf("%d",&n);
x = n;
for ( k = 1 ; k <= n ; k++ )
{
for ( c = 1 ; c <= k ; c++ )
{
printf("%d",num);
num++;
}
num--;
for ( c = 1 ; c <= 2*x - 3 ; c++ )
printf(" ");
x--;
if ( k != n )
{
for ( c = 1 ; c <= k ; c++ )
{
printf("%d",num);
num--;
}
}
else
{
num--;
for ( c = 1 ; c <= k - 1 ; c++ )
{
printf("%d",num);
num--;
}
}
printf("\n");
```

```
num = 1;
}
getch();
return 0;
}
```

Program -122] To Print Pattern

```
1
232
34543
4567654
567898765
#include<stdio.h>
#include<conio.h>
main()
{
int n, c, d, num = 1, space;
clrscr();
printf("Enter the level:");
scanf("%d",&n);
space = n - 1;
for ( d = 1 ; d <= n ; d++ )
{
num = d;
for ( c = 1 ; c <= space ; c++ )
printf(" ");
space--;
for ( c = 1 ; c <= d ; c++ )
{
printf("%d", num);
num++;
}
num--;
num--;
for ( c = 1 ; c < d ; c++)
{
printf("%d", num);
```

```
num--;
}
printf("\n");
}
getch();
return 0;
}
```

Program -123] To Print Pattern.

```
*******
*** ***
** **
* *
#include<stdio.h>
#include<conio.h>
main()
{
int n, c, k, space, r;
clrscr();
printf("Enter number of rows:");
scanf("%d",&n);
space = 1;
r = n-1;
for( c = 1 ; c <= 2*n - 1 ; c++ )
printf("*");
printf("\n");
for ( k = 2 ; k <= n ; k++ )
{
for( c = 1 ; c <= r ; c++ )
printf("*");
for ( c = 1 ; c <= space ; c++ )
printf(" ");
space = 2*k-1;
for( c = 1 ; c <= r ; c++ )
printf("*");
r--;
printf("\n");
```

```
}
getch();
return 0;
}
```

Program -124] To Print Pattern.

```
*
**
***
****
*****
```

```
#include<stdio.h>
#include<conio.h>
main()
{
int n, c, k, space;
clrscr();
printf("Enter number of rows:");
scanf("%d",&n);
space = n;
for ( k = 1 ; k <= n ; k++ )
{
for ( c = 1 ; c < space ; c++ )
printf(" ");
space--;
for( c = 1 ; c <= k ; c++ )
printf("*");
printf("\n");
}
getch();
return 0;
}
```

Program -125] Program to generate following output.

```
1
2 2
```

3 3 3
4 4 4 4
5 5 5 5 5
6 6 6 6 6 6
7 7 7 7 7 7 7

```
#include<stdio.h>
#include<conio.h>
main()
{
int i,j;
clrscr();
for(i=1;i<=10;i++)
{
for(j=1;j<=i;j++)
printf("%4d",i);
printf("\n");
}
getch();
return(0);
}
```

Program -126] Program to print n lines of Floyd's triangle.

1
2 3
4 5 6
7 8 9 10

```
#include<stdio.h>
#include<conio.h>
main()
{
int n,i,j,a=1;
clrscr();
printf("\n Enter no of lines:");
scanf("%d",&n);
for(i=1;i<=n;i++)
{
for(j=1;j<=i;j++)
```

```
{
printf("%4d",a);
a+=1;
}
printf("\n");
}
getch();
return(0);
}
```

Program -127] To Print Pattern.

```
*
**
***
****
***
**
*
#include<stdio.h>
#include<conioh>
main()
{
int n, c, k;
clrscr();
printf("Enter number of rows:");
scanf("%d",&n);
for ( c = 1 ; c <= n ; c++)
{
for ( k = 1 ; k <= c ; k++ )
printf("*");
printf("\n");
}
for ( c = n - 2 ; c >= 0 ; c-- )
{
for ( k = c ; k >= 0 ; k-- )
printf("*");
printf("\n");
```

```
}
getch();
return 0;
}
```

Program -128] To Print Pattern.

```
*
*A*
*A*A*
*A*A*A*
#include<stdio.h>
#include<conio.h>
main()
{
int n, c, k, space, count = 1;
clrscr();
printf("Enter number of rows:");
scanf("%d",&n);
space = n;
for ( c = 1 ; c <= n ; c++)
{
for( k = 1 ; k < space ; k++)
printf(" ");
for ( k = 1 ; k <= c ; k++)
{
printf("*");
if ( c > 1 && count < c)
{
printf("A");
count++;
}
}
printf("\n");
space--;
count = 1;
}
getch();
```

```
return 0;
}
```

Program -129] Program to print the following output.

```
* * * * *
* * * *
* * *
* *
*
#include<stdio.h>
#include<conio.h>
main()
{
int i,j,k,row,col;
clrscr();
printf("Input the no of rows:");
scanf("%d",&row);
printf("Output the no of columns:");
scanf("%d",&col);
for(i=0;i<row;i++,col--)
{
for(j=0;j<col;j++)
{
printf("*\t");
}
printf("\n");
for(k=0;k<=i;k++)
printf("");
}
getch();
return(0);
}
```

Program -130] Program to print the following pattern.

```
*
* *
```

```
* * *
* * * *
* * * * *
#include<stdio.h>
#include<conio.h>
main()
{
int i,j;
clrscr();
for(i=1;i<=5;i++)
{
for(j=1;j<=i;j++)
printf(" * ");
printf("\n");
}
getch();
return(0);
}
```

Program -131] Program to print following pattern.

```
1
1 2
1 2 3
1 2 3 4
1 2 3 4 5
#include<stdio.h>
#include<conio.h>
main()
{
int i,j;
clrscr();
for(i=1;i<=5;i++)
{
for(j=1;j<=i;j++)
printf("%3d",j);
printf("\n");
}
```

```
getch();
return(0);
}
```

Program -132] Program to print the following output.

```
*
* *
* * *
* * * *
#include<stdio.h>
#include<conio.h>
main()
{
int i,j,k,f1,f2,f3,z,sp,t;
char ans='*';
sp=20;
clrscr();
for(i=0;i<=4;i++)
{
for(k=0;k<sp-i;k++)
printf(" ");
sp-=2;
for(j=0;j<=i;j++)
{
f1=f2=f3=1;
t=i;
while(t!=0)
{
f1=f1*t;
t--;
}
t=j;
while(t!=0)
{
f2=f2*t;
t--;
}
```

```
t=i-j;
while(t!=0)
{
f3=f3*t;
t--;
}
printf("%6c",ans);
}
printf("\n");
}
getch();
return(0);
}
```

Program -133] Program to print following output.

```
A B C D E F G F E D C B A
A B C D E F F E D C B A
A B C D E E D C B A
A B C D D C B A
A B C C B A
A B B A
A A
#include<stdio.h>
#include<conio.h>
void main()
{
int l,m,n=0;
char i,j,k;
clrscr();
for(i=71;i>=65;i--)
{
for(j=65;j<=i;j++)
printf("%3c",j);
if(i==71)
m=70;
else
{
```

```
m=i;
for(l=0;l<=n-4;l++)
printf(" ");
}
for(k=m;k>=65;k--)
printf("%3c",k);
printf("\n");
n+=6;
}
getch();
}
```

Program -134] To Print Pattern.

```
EDCBA
DCBA
CBA
BA
A
#include<stdio.h>
#include<conio.h>
main()
{
int n, c, k, space = 0;
char ch, temp;
clrscr();
printf("Enter the level:");
scanf("%d",&n);
ch = 'A'+n-1;
temp = ch;
for ( k = n ; k >= 1 ; k-- )
{
for ( c = 1 ; c <= space; c++)
printf(" ");
space++;
for ( c = 1 ; c <= k ; c++ )
{
printf("%c",temp);
```

```
temp--;
}
printf("\n");
ch--;
temp = ch;
}
getch();
return 0;
}
```

Program -135] To Print Pattern.

```
A
B B
C C C
D D D D
E E E E E
#include<stdio.h>
#include<conio.h>
main()
{
int c, n, k;
char ch = 'A';
clrscr();
printf("Enter number of rows:");
scanf("%d",&n);
for ( c = 1 ; c <= n ; c++ )
{
for ( k = 1 ; k <= c ; k++)
printf("%c ", ch);
printf("\n");
ch++;
}
getch();
return 0;
}
```

Program -136] Program to print Pascal Traingle.

```
1
1 1
1 2 1
1 3 3 1
#include<stdio.h>
#include<conio.h>
main()
{
int i,j,k,f1,f2,f3,z,sp,t;
sp=20;
clrscr();
for(i=0;i<=4;i++)
{
for(k=0;k<sp-i;k++)
printf(" ");
sp-=2;
for(j=0;j<=i;j++)
{
f1=f2=f3=1;
t=i;
while(t!=0)
{
f1=f1*t;
t--;
}
t=j;
while(t!=0)
{
f2=f2*t;
t--;
}
t=i-j;
while(t!=0)
{
f3=f3*t;
t--;
}
```

```
z=f1/(f2*f3);
printf("%6d",z);
}
printf("\n");
}
getch();
return(0);
}
```

Program -137] Program to print following Output.

```
1
121
12321
1234321
123454321
12345654321
1234567654321
```

```
#include<stdio.h>
#include<conio.h>
main()
{
int r,i,j;
clrscr();
for(r=1;r<=10;r++)
{
for(i=1;i<=10-r+1;i++)
printf(" ");
for(i=1;i<=r;i++)
printf("%d",i%10);
for(j=i-2;j>=1;j--)
printf("%d",j%10);
printf("\n");
}
getch();
return(0);
}
```

Program -138] To Print Pattern.

```
Z Y X W X Y Z
Z Y X Y Z
Z Y Z
Z
#include<stdio.h>
#include<conio.h>
void main()
{
int i,row,j,k,l;
char ch='Z';
clrscr();
j=4;
for(i=1;i<=4;i++)
{
for(row=1;row<=i;row++)
printf(" ");
for(k=1;k<=j;k++)
{
printf("%2c",ch);
ch--;
}
k--;
ch++;
for(l=1;l<k;l++)
{
ch++;
printf("%2c",ch);
}
printf("\n");
j--;
}
getch();
}
```

Program -139] To Print Pattern.

```
A
A B
A B C
A B C D
A B C D E
#include<stdio.h>
#include<conio.h>
void main()
{
char i,j;
clrscr();
for(i=65;i<=69;i++)
{
for(j=65;j<=i;j++)
printf("%2c",j);
printf("\n");
}
getch();
}
```

Program -140] Program to print pattern.

```
1
1 2
1 2 3
1 2 3 4
1 2 3 4 5
1 2 3 4
1 2 3
1 2
1
#include<stdio.h>
#include<conio.h>
void main()
{
int i,j;
clrscr();
for(i=1;i<=5;i++)
```

```
{
for(j=1;j<=i;j++)
printf("%4d",j);
printf("\n");
}
for(i=4;i>=1;i--)
{
for(j=1;j<=i;j++)
printf("%4d",j);
printf("\n");
}
getch();
}
```

Program -141] Program Print Following Pattern.

```
1
1 2
1 2 3
1 2 3 4
1 2 3 4 5
#include <stdio.h>
#include <conio.h>
int main()
{
int i,j,n,space;
clrscr();
printf("Enter how many rows ?");
scanf("%d",&n);
for(i=1; i<=n; i++)
{
for(space=n; space>=i; space--)
{
printf(" ");
}
for(j=1; j<=i; j++)
{
printf("%2d",j);
```

```
}
printf("\n");
}
getch();
return(0);
}
```

Program -142] Program Print Following Pattern.

```
*
**
***
****
*****
*****
****
***
**
*
#include<stdio.h>
#include<conio.h>
main()
{
int n, c, k, space;
clrscr();
printf("Enter number of rows:");
scanf("%d",&n);
space = n;
for (k=1;k<=n;k++)
{
for (c=1;c<space;c++)
printf(" ");
space--;
for( c = 1 ; c <= k ; c++ )
printf("*");
printf("\n");
}
space=1;
```

```
for (k=n;k>=1;k--)
{
for (c=1;c<n;c++)
printf(" ");
space++;
for( c=1;c<=k;c++)
printf("*");
printf("\n");
}
getch();
return 0;
}
```

Program -143] Program Print Following Pattern.

```
*
**
***
****
*****
*****
****
***
**
*
```

```
#include<stdio.h>
#include<conio.h>
main()
{
int n, c, k, space;
clrscr();
printf("Enter number of rows:");
scanf("%d",&n);
space = n;
for (k=1;k<=n;k++)
{
for (c=1;c<space;c++)
printf(" ");
```

```
space--;
for( c = 1 ; c <= k ; c++ )
printf("*");
printf("\n");
}
for (k=n;k>=1;k--)
{
for (c=1;c>n;c--)
printf(" ");
space++;
for( c=1;c<=k;c++)
printf("*");
printf("\n");
}
getch();
return 0;
}
```

Program -144] Program Print Following Pattern.

```
#
##
###
####
#####
####
###
##
#
#include <stdio.h>
#include <conio.h>
int main()
{
int i,j,a,n,space=1;
clrscr();
printf ("Enter how many rows ?");
scanf ("%d",&n);
for(i=1; i<=n; i++)
```

```
{
for(a=space; a<=n; a++)
{
printf(" ");
}
for(j=0; j< i; j++)
{
printf("#");
}
space = space + 1;
printf("\n");
}
space = 1;
for(i=n-1; i>=1; i--)
{
for(a=space; a>=0; a--)
{
printf(" ");
}
for(j=i; j>=1; j--)
{
printf("#");
}
space = space + 1;
printf("\n");
}
getch();
return(0);
}
```

Program -145] Program Print Following Pattern.

```
#####
####
###
##
#
#include <stdio.h>
#include <conio.h>
int main()
```

```
{
int i,j,a,n,space=1;
clrscr();
printf("Enter How many rows ?");
scanf("%d",&n);
for(i=n; i>=1; i--)
{
for(a=space; a>=0; a--)
{
printf(" "); // only 1 space
}
for(j=i; j>=1; j--)
{
printf("#");
}
space = space + 1;
printf("\n");
}
getch();
return(0);
}
```

Program -146] Program Print Following Pattern.

```
1
2 2
3 3 3
4 4 4 4
#include <stdio.h>
#include <conio.h>
void main()
{
int i,n,a,p,q;
clrscr();
printf("Enter how many rows ?");
scanf("%d",&n);
q=n;
for(i=1;i<=n;i++)
```

```
{
for(a=1;a<=q;a++)
{
printf(" ");
}
for(p=1;p<=i;p++)
{
printf("%d",i);
printf(" ");
}
printf("\n");
q=q-1;
}
getch();
}
```

Program -147] Program Print Following Pattern.

```
5
4 4
3 3 3
2 2 2 2
1 1 1 1 1
#include <stdio.h>
#include <conio.h>
void main()
{
int i,n,a,p,q;
clrscr();
printf("Enter how many rows ?");
scanf("%d",&n);
q=n;
for(i=1;i<=n;i++)
{
for(a=1;a<=q;a++)
{
printf(" ");
}
```

```
for(p=1;p<=i;p++)
{
printf("%d",i);
printf(" ");
}
printf("\n");
q=q-1;
}
getch();
}
```

CHAPTER EIGHT

Sum Of Series Programs

Program -148] Program calculate sum of series 1+2+3+4+________+100.

```
#include<stdio.h>
#include<conio.h>
void main()
{
int n=1,sum=0;
clrscr();
while(n<=100)
{
sum=sum+n;
n++;
}
printf("\nThe sum of series is: %d",sum);
getch();
}
```

Output:

The sum of series is: 5050

Program -149] Calculate value of sum of series 1!+2!+3!+....+10!.

```
#include<stdio.h>
#include<conio.h>
void main()
{
int n,i,j;
long fact=1,sum=0;
clrscr();
for(j=1;j<=10;j++)
```

```
{
fact=1;
for(i=1;i<=j;i++)
fact=fact*i;
sum=sum+fact;
printf("Factorial of %d is:%ld\n",j,fact);
}
printf("\n\nThe value of ");
for(i=1;i<=10;i++)
printf("%d!+",i);
printf(" is=%ld",sum);
getch();
}
```

Output:

Factorial of 1 is:1
Factorial of 2 is:2
Factorial of 3 is:6
Factorial of 4 is:24
Factorial of 5 is:120
Factorial of 6 is:720
Factorial of 7 is:5040
Factorial of 8 is:40320
Factorial of 9 is:362880
Factorial of 10 is:3628800
The value of 1!+2!+3!+4!+5!+6!+7!+8!+9!+10!+ is=4037913

Program -150] Calculate value of sum of series 1-1/3+1/5-1/7+1/9....up to 10 terms.

```
#include<stdio.h>
#include<conio.h>
void main()
{
int i,j=-2;
float sum=0,n=1;
clrscr();
for(i=1;i<=10;i++)
```

```
{
printf("\t%f",n);
sum+=1/(float)n;
n=-n+j;
j=-j;
}
printf("\n\nSum of series is:%f",sum);
getch();
}
```

Output:

```
1.00
-3.00
5.00
-7.00
9.00
-11.00
13.00
-15.00
17.00
-19.00
Sum of series is:0.760460
```

Program -151] Program calculate value of sum of series. 1/1!+1/2!+1/3!+1/5!.

```
#include<stdio.h>
#include<conio.h>
void main()
{
int n,i,j;
float sum=0;
long int fact=1;
clrscr();
for(n=1;n<=5;n++)
{
fact=1;
for(i=1;i<=n;i++)
fact=fact*i;
```

```
sum+=1/(float)fact;
}
printf("\n\nThe value of ");
for(i=1;i<=5;i++)
printf("1/%d!+",i);
printf(" is=%f",sum);
getch();
}
```

Output:

The value of 1/1!+1/2!+1/3!+1/4!+1/5!+ is=1.716667

Program -152] Program calculate value of sum of series 1/1!-1/3!+1/5!-1/7!+1/9!....up to 10.

```
#include<stdio.h>
#include<conio.h>
void main()
{
int i,j=-2,k;
float sum=0,n=1,l=1;
long int fact=1;
clrscr();
printf("Term \t Factorial\n");
for(i=1;i<=10;i++)
{
fact=1;
for(k=1;k<=l;k++)
fact=fact*k;
if(n<0)
fact=-fact;
printf("\n%.2f\t%ld",n,fact);
sum+=1/(float)fact;
n=-n+j;
l=0;
if(n<0)
l=-n;
else
l=n;
```

```
j=-j;
}
printf("\n\nSum of series is:%f",sum);
getch();
}
```

Output:

```
Term Factorial
1.00 1
-3.00 -6
5.00 120
-7.00 -5040
9.00 362880
-11.00 -39916800
13.00 1932053504
-15.00 -2004310016
17.00 -288522240
-19.00 -109641728
Sum of series is:0.841471
```

Program -153] Calculate value of sum of series 1!-3!+5!-7!+9!....up to 10 terms.

```
#include<stdio.h>
#include<conio.h>
void main()
{
int i,j=-2,k;
float sum=0,n=1,l=1;
long int fact=1;
clrscr();
printf("Term \t Factorial\n");
for(i=1;i<=10;i++)
{
fact=1;
for(k=1;k<=l;k++)
fact=fact*k;
if(n<0)
fact=-fact;
```

```
printf("\n%.2f\t%ld",n,fact);
sum+=(float)fact;
n=-n+j;
l=0;
if(n<0)
l=-n;
else
l=n;
j=-j;
}
printf("\n\nSum of series is:%f",sum);
getch();
}
```

Output:

```
Term Factorial
1.00 1
-3.00 -6
5.00 120
-7.00 -5040
9.00 362880
-11.00 -39916800
13.00 1932053504
-15.00 -2004310016
17.00 -288522240
-19.00 -109641728
Sum of series is:-509979264.000000
```

Program -154] Calculate value of sin(x).

```
#include<stdio.h>
#include<conio.h>
#include<math.h>
void main()
{
int x,n=1,i,j,sign=1;
long int fact=1;
float deg,sum=0,angle=1;
clrscr();
```

```
printf("\nx=");
scanf("%d",&x);
deg=x*3.14/180;
for(i=1;i<=10;i++)
{
fact=1;
angle=1;
for(i=1;i<=n;i++)
fact*=i;
fact=fact*sign;
for(i=1;i<=n;i++)
angle=angle*deg;
sum=sum+angle/(float)fact;
sign=-sign;
n+=2;
}
printf("\n\nSum of series is:%2f",sum);
getch();
}
```

Input:

x=1

Output:

Sum of series is:0.017444

Program -155] Program to calculate value of sum of series. x2/2!-x4/4!+x6/6!-x8/8!.

```
#include<stdio.h>
#include<conio.h>
void main()
{
int x,n=1,i,j,l=2;
long int fact=1;
float sum=0,prod=1;
clrscr();
printf("\nx=");
scanf("%d",&x);
```

```
n=2;
i=-2;
while(n<10)
{
fact=1;
prod=1;
for(j=1;j<=l;j++)
fact*=j;
if(n<0)
fact=-fact;
for(j=1;j<=l;j++)
prod=prod*x;
printf("\n%d\t%ld\t%f",n,fact,prod);
sum=sum+prod/(float)fact;
n=-n+i;
i=-i;
l=0;
if(n<0)
l=-n;
else
l=n;
}
printf("\n\nSum of series is:%2f",sum);
getch();
}
```

Input:

x=2

Output:

Term Fact Product
2 2 4.000000
-4 -24 16.000000
6 720 64.000000
-8 -40320 256.000000
Sum of series is:1.415873

Program -156] Program to print series 2 -4 6 -8 10 -12 14.....20.

```
#include<stdio.h>
```

```
#include<conio.h>
void main()
{
int n,i,j;
clrscr();
n=2;
i=-2;
while(n<20)
{
printf("%4d",n);
n=-n+i;
i=-i;
}
getch();
}
```

Output:

2 -4 6 -8 10 -12 14 -16 18 -20

Program -157] Program calculate value of natural logarithm.

x-1/x + ½(x-1/x)2 + ½ (x-1/x)3 + ½ (x-1/x)4 +...

```
#include<stdio.h>
#include<conio.h>
#include<math.h>
void main()
{
int a,j;
float ans=0;
clrscr();
printf("\n Enter the value of x:");
scanf("%d",&a);
for(j=1;j<=7;j++)
{
if(j==1)
ans=ans+pow((a-1.0)/a,j);
else
ans=ans+(1.0/2)*pow((a-1.0)/a,j);
}
```

```
printf("\n Log(%d)=%f",a,ans);
getch();
}
```

Input:

Enter the value of x:1

Output:

Log(1)=0.000000

Program -158] Program to compute COSINE Series cos(x)=1-x^2/2!+x^4/4!-x^6/6!+...x^n/n!*/

```
#include<stdio.h>
#include<conio.h>
#include<math.h>
void main()
{
float x,a,cossum;
int i,n=20;
clrscr();
printf("\nEnter the value of cos(x):");
scanf("%f",&x);
x=(float)x*3.14/(float)180;
a =1;
cossum =1;
for(i=1;i<n+1;i++)
{
a = a *pow((double)(-1),(double)(2*i-1))*x*x/(2*i*(2*i-1));
cossum = cossum + a;
}
printf("\ncox(x)=%f", cossum);
getch();
}
```

Input:

Enter the value of cos(x):0

Output:

cox(x)=1.000000

CHAPTER NINE

Switch Statement

Program -159] Program to check vowels using Switch Case Statement.

```
#include<stdio.h>
#include<conio.h>
void main()
{
char ch;
clrscr();
printf("Enter a character:");
scanf("%c",&ch);
switch(ch)
{
case ‘a’:
case ‘A’:
case ‘e’:
case ‘E’:
case ‘i’:
case ‘I’:
case ‘o’:
case ‘O’:
case ‘u’:
case ‘U’:
printf("%c is a vowel.\n", ch);
break;
default:
printf("%c is not a vowel.\n", ch);
}
getch();
}
```

Input:
Enter a character:a
Output:
a is a vowel.

Program -160] Program to convert numbers into words.

```
#include<stdio.h>
#include<conio.h>
void main()
{
int ch;
clrscr();
printf("Enter a number (1 to 10):");
scanf("%d",&ch);
switch(ch)
{
case 1:
printf("One");
break;
case 2:
printf("Two");
break;
case 3:
printf("Three");
break;
case 4:
printf("Four");
break;
case 5:
printf("Five");
break;
case 6:
printf("Six");
break;
case 7:
printf("Seven");
break;
```

```
case 8:
printf("Eight");
break;
case 9:
printf("Nine");
break;
case 10:
printf("Ten");
break;
case 0:
printf("exit");
break;
}
getch();
}
```

Input:

Enter a number (1 to 10):9

Output:

Nine

Program -161] Program to convert decimal number into its equivalent binary,

octal and hexadecimal.

```
#include<stdio.h>
#include<conio.h>
void main()
{
int ch,n,i=1,bin[10],oct[10],hex[10],j;
clrscr();
printf("\n1.Binary");
printf("\n2.Octal");
printf("\n3.Hexadecimal");
printf("\nEnter any choice:");
scanf("%d",&ch);
switch(ch)
{
case 1:
```

```
printf("\nEnter any number:");
scanf("%d",&n);
while(n>0)
{
bin[i]=n%2;
n=n/2;
i++;
}
printf("\nBinary equivalent is:");
for(j=i-1;j>=1;j--)
printf("%d",bin[j]);
break;
case 2:
printf("\nEnter any number:");
scanf("%d",&n);
while(n>0)
{
oct[i]=n%8;
n=n/8;
i++;
}
printf("\nOctal equivalent is:");
for(j=i-1;j>=1;j--)
printf("%d",oct[i]);
break;
case 3:
printf("\nEnter any number:");
scanf("%d",&n);
while(n>0)
{
hex[i]=n%16;
n=n/16;
i++;
}
printf("\nHexadecimal equivalent is:");
for(j=i-1;j>=1;j--)
{
switch(hex[j])
```

```
{
case 10:
printf("A");
break;
case 11:
printf("B");
break;
case 12:
printf("C");
break;
case 13:
printf("D");
break;
case 14:
printf("E");
break;
case 15:
printf("F");
break;
default:
printf("%d",hex[i]);
break;
}
}
break;
default:
printf("\nWrong choice");
}
getch();
}
```

Output:

```
1.Binary
2.Octal
3.Hexadecimal
Enter any choice:1
Enter any number:8
Binary equivalent is:1000
```

Program -162] Program to calculate factorial, no is Prime or not, no is even or odd using switch case.

```
#include<stdio.h>
#include<conio.h>
void main()
{
int ch,n,i;
long int fact;
clrscr();
while(1)
{
printf("\n\n1.Factorial");
printf("\n2.Prime Number");
printf("\n3.Even/Odd");
printf("\n0.Exit");
printf("\nEnter choice:");
scanf("%d",&ch);
switch(ch)
{
case 1:
printf("\nEnter number:");
scanf("%d",&n);
fact=1;
for(i=1;i<=n;i++)
fact=fact*i;
printf("\nFactorial is:%lu",fact);
break;
case 2:
printf("\nEnter number:");
scanf("%d",&n);
for(i=2;i<n;i++)
{
if(n%i==0)
{
printf("\nNot prime number.");
break;
```

```
}
}
if(i==n)
printf("\nPrime number");
break;
case 3:
printf("\nEnter number:");
scanf("%d",&n);
if(n%2==0)
printf("\nEven Number");
else
printf("\nOdd Number");
break;
case 0:
exit();
break;
}
}
}
```

Output:

```
1.Factorial
2.Prime Number
3.Even/Odd
0.Exit
Enter choice:1
Enter number:5
Factorial is:120
1.Factorial
2.Prime Number
3.Even/Odd
0.Exit
Enter choice:2
Enter number:2
Prime number
1.Factorial
2.Prime Number
3.Even/Odd
0.Exit
```

Enter choice:3
Enter number:2
Even Number
1.Factorial
2.Prime Number
3.Even/Odd
0.Exit
Enter choice:0

CHAPTER TEN

Function Programs

Program -163] Program to Swap Values using Call By Reference.

```
#include<stdio.h>
#include<conio.h>
void swap(int*, int*);
void main()
{
int x, y;
clrscr();
printf("Enter the value of x and y.");
printf("\nx:");
scanf("%d",&x);
printf("\ny:");
scanf("%d",&y);
printf("\nBefore Swapping\nx = %d\ny = %d\n", x, y);
swap(&x, &y);
printf("\nAfter Swapping\nx = %d\ny = %d\n", x, y);
getch();
}
void swap(int *a, int *b)
{
int temp;
temp = *b;
*b = *a;
*a = temp;
}
```

Input:

```
Enter the value of x and y.
x:8
```

y:9

Output:

Before Swapping

x = 8

y = 9

After Swapping

x = 9

y = 8

Program -164] Write a function power(a,b) to calculate the value of a raised to b.

```
#include<stdio.h>
#include<conio.h>
void main()
{
int a,b;
long pow,power();
clrscr();
printf("\n Enter the base number:");
scanf("%d",&a);
printf("\n Enter the power number:");
scanf("%d",&b);
pow=power(a,b);
printf("\n%d raised to the power %d is = %d",a,b,pow);
getch();
}
long power(int x,int y)
{
int j;
long q=1;
for(j=1;j<=b;j++)
q=q*a;
return(q);
}
```

Input:

Enter the base number:2

Enter the power number:3

Output:

2 raised to the power 3 is = 8

Program -165] Program to calculate factorial value of an integer using a function.

```
#include<stdio.h>
#include<conio.h>
void main()
{
int n;
long factorial,fact();
clrscr();
printf("\n Enter a number:");
scanf("%d",&n);
factorial=fact(n);
printf("\n Factorial of %d is %d",n,factorial);
getch();
}
long fact(int n)
{
int k;
long factorial=1;
for(k=1;k<=n;k++)
factorial=factorial*k;
return(factorial);
}
```

Input:

Enter a number:6

Output:

Factorial of 6 is 720

Program -166] Program to find out whether a year is leap or not using function.

```
#include<stdio.h>
#include<conio.h>
void leapyr(int);
```

```
void main()
{
int yr;
clrscr();
printf("\nEnter year:");
scanf("%d",&yr);
leapyr(yr);
getch();
}
void leapyr(int yr)
{
if(yr%4==0 && yr%100!=0||yr%400==0)
printf("\n%d is leap year",yr);
else
printf("\n%d is not leap year",yr);
}
```

Input:

Enter year:2016

Output:

2016 is leap year

Program -167] Program to convert given year into its roman equivalent.

```
#include<stdio.h>
#include<conio.h>
void main()
{
int year;
clrscr();
printf("\nEnter year:");
scanf("%d",&year);
year=roman(year,1000,'m');
year=roman(year,500,'d');
year=roman(year,100,'c');
year=roman(year,50,'l');
year=roman(year,10,'x');
year=roman(year,5,'v');
year=roman(year,1,'i');
```

```
getch();
}
roman(int y,int k,char ch)
{
int p,q;
if(y==9)
{
printf("ix");
return(y%9);
}
if(y==4)
{
printf("iv");
return(y%4);
}
q=y/k;
for(p=1;p<=q;p++)
printf("%c",ch);
return(y-k*q);
}
```

Input:

Enter year:2012

Output:

mmxii

Program -168] Program to obtain prime factors of a number.

```
#include<stdio.h>
#include<conio.h>
void primefact(int);
void main()
{
int n;
clrscr();
printf("\nEnter number:");
scanf("%d",&n);
primefact (n);
getch();
```

```
}
void primefact (int n)
{
int i=2;
printf("\nPrime factors of %d are: ",n);
while(n!=1)
{
if(n%i==0)
printf("%4d",i);
else
{
i++;
continue;
}
n=n/i;
}
}
```

Input:

Enter number:12

Output: Prime factors of 12 are: 2 2 3

Program -169] Find prime factors of number recursively.

```
#include<stdio.h>
#include<conio.h>
void main()
{
int no;
clrscr();
printf("\nEnter number:");
scanf("%d",&no);
printf("Prime factors are:");
factor(no);
getch();
}
factor(int num)
{
static int i=2;
```

```
if(i<=num)
{
if(num%i==0)
{
printf("%4d",i);
num=num/i;
}
else
i++;
factor(num);
}
return;
}
```

Input:

Enter number:24

Output:

Prime factors are: 2 2 2 3

Program -170] Find Binary equivalent of a decimal number.

```
#include<stdio.h>
#include<conio.h>
void main()
{
int no;
clrscr();
printf("\nEnter the number:");
scanf("%d",&no);
binary(no);
getch();
}
binary(int num)
{
int rem;
rem=num%2;
num=num/2;
if(num==0)
{
```

```
printf("\nThe equivalent is %d",rem);
return(rem);
}
else
binary(num);
printf("%d",rem);
return(rem);
}
```

Input:

Enter the number:23

Output:

The equivalent is 10111

Program -171] Program to check Vowels using function.

```
#include<stdio.h>
#include<conio.h>
void main()
{
char ch;
int ans;
clrscr();
printf("Enter the character:");
scanf("%c",&ch);
ans=check_vowel(ch);
if(ans==1)
printf("The %c is a vowal.",ch);
else
printf("The %c is not a vowal.",ch);
getch();
}
int check_vowel(char a)
{
if ( a >= 'A' && a <= 'Z' )
a = a + 'a' - 'A'; /* Converting to lower case */
if ( a == 'a' || a == 'e' || a == 'i' || a == 'o' || a == 'u')
return 1;
return 0;
```

```
}
```

Input:

Enter the character:i

Output:

The i is a vowel.

Program -172] Program Two functions calling the same function.

```
#include<stdio.h>
#include<conio.h>
float square (float a);
void main()
{
float numerator(float x,float y);
float denominator(float x, float y);
float x,y,result;
clrscr();
printf("\nEnter the value of x:");
scanf("%f",&x);
printf("\nEnter the value of y:");
scanf("%f",&y);
result=numerator(x,y)/denominator(x,y);
printf("Result:%f",result);
getch();
}
float numerator(float x, float y)
{
float temp;
temp=square(x)+square(y);
return(temp);
}
float denominator(float x, float y)
{
float temp;
temp=square(x)-square(y);
return(temp);
}
float square(float a)
```

```
{
return (a*a);
}
```

Input:

Enter the value of x:6

Enter the value of y:3

Output:

Result:1.666667

Program -173] Program to recognise type of shape.

```
#include<stdio.h>
#include<conio.h>
void main()
{
void shape(int,...);
clrscr();
shape(2,5,10);
shape(4,1,1,10,1);
shape(6,15,10,5,25,20,25);
}
void shape(int totpoint,...)
{
switch(totpoint)
{
case 2:
printf("\nType of shape is point");
break;
case 4:
printf("\nType of shape is line");
break;
case 6:
printf("\nType of shape is triangle");
break;
}
getch();
}
```

CHAPTER ELEVEN

C Preprocessor Programs

Program -174] Macros like ISUPPER,ISLOWER,ISALPHA,BIG.

```
#include<stdio.h>
#include<conio.h>
#define ISUCASE(a)(a>=65 && a<=90?1:0)
#define ISLCASE(a)(a>=97 && a<=122?1:0)
#define ISALCASE(a)(ISUPPER(a)||ISLOWER(a))
#define MAX(a,b)(a>b?a:b)
void main()
{
char ch;
int l,x,y;
clrscr();
printf("\nEnter any Character:");
scanf("%c",&ch);
if(ISUCASE(ch)==1)
printf("\n\n Entered letter is capital");
else if(ISLCASE(ch)==1)
printf("\n\n Entered letter is small case");
else if(ISALCASE(ch)!=1)
printf("\n\n Entered character is other than alphabet");
printf("\nEnter any two no:");
scanf("%d%d",&x,&y);
l=BIG(x,y);
printf("\nBigger no is %d",l);
getch();
}
```

Input:

Enter any alphabet/character:a

Output:

You entered a small case letter

Input:

Enter any two no:

Number 1 5

Output:

Bigger no is 5

Program -175] Calculate area, circumference of circle and area of square using macros.

Of header file.

Step-1 Create area.h file in “tc\Include\area.h” folder

Write down following three macros. Save and close file.

```
#define ACIRCLE(r) (3.14*r*r)
#define CIRCIRCLE(r) (2*3.14*r)
#define ASQ(s) (s*s)
```

Step-2 Include this file in program as a header file given below.

```
#include<stdio.h>
#include<conio.h>
#include "area.h"
void main()
{
char ch;
int r;
float a,c,s,sa;
clrscr();
printf("\n Enter radius of circle :");
scanf("%d",&r);
a = ACIRCLE(r);
c = CIRCIRCLE(r);
printf("\n Area of circle is %f :",a);
printf("\n Circumference of circle is %f ",c);
printf("\n Enter side of square :");
scanf("%f",&s);
sa = ASQ(s);
printf("\n Area of square is %f ",sa);
getch();
```

```
}
```

Program -176] Macros like ABS,TOLOWER.

```
#include<stdio.h>
#include<conio.h>
#define ABS(x)(x<0?x*-1:x)
#define TOLOWER(x)(x+32)
void main()
{
char ch;
int d,a,b,c;
clrscr();
printf("\n\nEnter any number:");
scanf("%d",&a);
d=ABS(a);
printf("\nAbsolute value is %d",d);
fflush(stdin);
printf("\n\nEnter any upper case character:");
scanf("%c",&ch);
ch=TOLOWER(ch);
printf("\nLower case character is %c",ch);
getch();
}
```

Output:

Enter any number:53.63
Absolute value is 53
Enter any upper case character:A
Lower case character is a

CHAPTER TWELVE

Array – One Dimensional

Program -177] Find maximum element from given array.

```
#include<stdio.h>
#include<conio.h>
void main()
{
int i,arr[10],max=0,n;
clrscr();
printf("\nEnter number of elements:");
scanf("%d", &n);
printf("\nEnter %d integers\n", n);
for(i=1;i<=n;i++)
scanf("%d",&arr[i]);
for(i=1;i<=n;i++)
{
if(arr[i]>max)
max=arr[i];
}
printf("\nThe element %d is maximum.",max);
getch();
}
```

Input:

Enter number of elements:5
Enter 5 integers
8
9
6
3
5

Output:
The element 9 is maximum.

Program -178] Program to find smallest and largest no from 10 nos.

```
#include<stdio.h>
#include<conio.h>
void main()
{
int a[10],i,max,min;
clrscr();
printf("\nEnter 10 elements:\n");
for(i=1;i<=10;i++)
scanf("%d",&a[i]);
for(i=1;i<=10;i++)
{
if(a[i] < min)
min = a[i];
if(a[i] > max)
max = a[i];
}
printf("\n Smallest no is: %d",min);
printf("\n Largest no is: %d",max);
getch();
}
```

Input:
Enter 10 elements:
2 5 64 8 9 5 2 31 2 4

Output:
Smallest no is: 2
Largest no is: 64

Program -179] Enter single dimensional array & calculate sum of element & average.

```
#include<stdio.h>
#include<conio.h>
```

```
void main()
{
int i,arr[10],sum=0,n;
float avg;
clrscr();
printf("Enter how many element do you want? Please enter below :");
scanf("%d",&n);
printf("Enter the element:\n");
for(i=1;i<=n;i++)
scanf("%d",&arr[i]);
for(i=1;i<=n;i++)
sum=sum+arr[i];
avg=(float)sum/n;
printf("\nThe sum of array element is: %d",sum);
printf("\nThe average of sum is: %0.2f ",avg);
getch();
}
```

Input:

Enter how many element do you want? Please enter below : 5
Enter the element:
1 2 3 4 5

Output:

The sum of array element is:15
The average of sum is:3.00

Program – 180] Print the single dimensional array.

```
#include<stdio.h>
#include<conio.h>
main()
{
int i,arr[5];
clrscr();
printf("Enter the five element:\n");
for(i=0;i<5;i++)
scanf("%d",&arr[i]);
printf("The array element’s are:");
for(i=0;i<5;i++)
```

```
{
printf("%d ",arr[i]);
}
getch();
return(0);
}
```

Input:

Enter the five element:

4 5 6 7 8

Output:

The array element's are:4 5 6 7 8

Program -181] Search a given element in Single Dimensional array.

```
#include<stdio.h>
#include<conio.h>
main()
{
int i,no,arr[5],cnt=0;
clrscr();
printf("Enter the five element in to array:\n");
for(i=0;i<5;i++)
scanf("%d",&arr[i]);
printf("\nEnter element want to search:");
scanf("%d",&no);
for(i=0;i<5;i++)
{
if(arr[i]==no)
cnt++;
}
printf("\nThe element %d is found in %d times",no,cnt);
getch();
return(0);
}
```

Input:

Enter the five element in to array:

4 5 6 6 3

Enter element want to search:6

Output:

The element 6 is found in 2 times

Program -182] Program to sort the single dimensional array in an ascending order.

```
#include<stdio.h>
#include<conio.h>
void main()
{
int i,j,temp,arr[5];
clrscr();
printf("\n Enter 5 nos:");
for(i=0;i<5;i++)
scanf("%d",&arr[i]);
for(i=0;i<5;i++)
{
for(j=0;j<5;j++)
{
if(arr[i]<arr[j])
{
temp = arr[i];
arr[i] = arr[j];
arr[j] = temp;
}
}
}
printf("\n Sorted array is \n");
for(j=0;j<5;j++)
printf("%d\n",arr[j]);
getch();
}
```

Input:

Enter 5 array element:

4 8 5 9 3

Output:

Sorted array is

3 4 5 8 9

Program -183] Program to sort the single dimentional array in an descending order.

```
#include<stdio.h>
#include<conio.h>
void main()
{
int i,j,temp,arr[5];
clrscr();
printf("\n Enter 5 nos:");
for(i=0;i<5;i++)
scanf("%d",&arr[i]);
for(i=0;i<5;i++)
{
for(j=0;j<5;j++)
{
if(arr[i]>arr[j])
{
temp = arr[i];
arr[i] = arr[j];
arr[j] = temp;
}
}
}
printf("\n Sorted array is \n");
for(j=0;j<5;j++)
printf("%d\n",arr[j]);
getch();
}
```

Input:

Enter 5 element of array:

4 8 6 2 9

Output:

Sorted array is

9 8 6 4 2

Program -184] Program print Array elements in reverse order.

```
#include<stdio.h>
#include<conio.h>
void main()
{
int n, i, d, temp, x[100], y[100];
clrscr();
printf("Enter the number of elements in array:");
scanf("%d",&n);
printf("\nEnter the array elements\n");
for ( i = 0 ; i < n ; i++ )
scanf("%d",&x[i]);
for ( i = n - 1, d = 0 ; i >= 0 ; i--, d++ )
y[d] = x[i];
for ( i = 0 ; i < n ; i++ )
x[i] = y[i];
printf("Reverse array is\n");
for( i = 0 ; i < n ; i++ )
printf("%d\n", x[i]);
getch();
}
```

Input:

Enter the number of elements in array:5

Enter the array elements

4 8 9 5 6

Output:

Reverse array is

6 5 9 8 4

Program -185] Search element using Linerar Search.

```
#include<stdio.h>
#include<conio.h>
void main()
{
int x[100], find, i, num;
clrscr();
```

```
printf("Enter the number of elements in array:");
scanf("%d",&num);
printf("\nEnter %d numbers\n", num);
for ( i = 0 ; i < num ; i++ )
scanf("%d",&x[i]);
printf("\nEnter the number to search:");
scanf("%d",&find);
for ( i = 0 ; i < num ; i++ )
{
if ( x[i] == find ) /* if required element found */
{
printf("%d is present at location %d.\n", find, i+1);
break;
}
}
if ( i == num )
printf("%d is not present in array.\n", find);
getch();
}
```

Input:

Enter the number of elements in array:5

Enter 5 numbers

8 6 4 9 3

Output:

Enter the number to search:9

9 is present at location 4.

Program -186] Search element using Binary Search.

```
#include<stdio.h>
#include<conio.h>
void main()
{
int i, n, find, x[100], bgn, end, mid;
clrscr();
printf("\nEnter number of elements:");
scanf("%d",&n);
printf("\nEnter %d integers:\n", n);
```

```
for ( i = 0 ; i < n ; i++ )
scanf("%d",&x[i]);
printf("\nEnter value to find:");
scanf("%d",&find);
bgn = 0;
end = n - 1;
mid = (bgn+end)/2;
while( bgn <= end )
{
if (x[mid] < find )
bgn = mid + 1;
else if ( x[mid] == find )
{
printf("\n%d found at location %d.\n", find, mid+1);
break;
}
else
end = mid - 1;
mid = (bgn + end)/2;
}
if ( bgn > end )
printf("\nNot found! %d is not present in the list.\n", find);
getch();
}
```

Input:

Enter number of elements:5

Enter 5 integers:

1 5 6 4 8

Enter value to find:5

Output:

5 found at location 2.

Program -187] Insert element in array

```
#include<stdio.h>
#include<conio.h>
void main()
{
```

```
int x[100], pos,i, n, no;
clrscr();
printf("\nEnter number of elements in array:");
scanf("%d", &n);
printf("\nEnter %d elements\n", n);
for ( i = 0 ; i < n ; i++ )
scanf("%d", &x[i]);
printf("\nEnter the location where element will be insert :");
scanf("%d", &pos);
printf("\nEnter the element to insert:");
scanf("%d", &no);
for ( i = n - 1 ; i >= pos - 1 ; i-- )
x[i+1] = x[i];
x[pos-1] = no;
printf("\nResultant array is\n");
for( i = 0 ; i <= n ; i++ )
printf("%d\n", x[i]);
getch();
}
```

Input:

Enter number of elements in array:5

Enter 5 elements

4 5 6 3 7

Enter the location where element will be insert :2

Enter the value to insert:9

Output:

Resultant array is

4 9 5 6 3 7

Program -188] Delete element from array.

```
#include<stdio.h>
#include<conio.h>
void main()
{
int x[100], pos, j, n;
clrscr();
printf("\nEnter number of elements in array:");
```

```
scanf("%d", &n);
printf("\nEnter %d elements\n", n);
for ( j = 0 ; j < n ; j++ )
scanf("%d", &x[j]);
printf("\nEnter the location where you wish to delete element:");
scanf("%d", &pos);
if ( pos >= n+1 )
printf("\nDeletion not possible.\n");
else
{
for ( j = pos - 1 ; j < n - 1 ; j++ )
x[j] = x[j+1];
printf("\nResultant array is\n");
for( j = 0 ; j < n - 1 ; j++ )
printf("%d\n", x[j]);
}
getch();
}
```

Input:

Enter number of elements in array:5

Enter 5 elements

7 8 9 6 3

Enter the location where you wish to delete element:4

Output:

Resultant array is

7 8 9 3

Program -189] Sorting method Bubble sort code.

```
#include<stdio.h>
#include<conio.h>
void main()
{
int x[100], no, i, d, temp;
clrscr();
printf("\nEnter number of elements:");
scanf("%d", &no);
printf("\nEnter %d integers\n", no);
```

```
for ( i = 0 ; i < no ; i++ )
scanf("%d", &x[i]);
for ( i = 0 ; i < ( no - 1 ) ; i++ )
{
for ( d = 0 ; d < no - i - 1 ; d++ )
{
if ( x[d] > x[d+1] )
{
temp = x[d];
x[d] = x[d+1];
x[d+1] = temp;
}
}
}
printf("\nSorted list in ascending order:\n");
for ( i = 0 ; i < no ; i++ )
printf("%d\n", x[i]);
getch();
}
```

Input:

Enter number of elements:5

Enter 5 integers

7 8 9 6 5

Output:

Sorted list in ascending order:

5 6 7 8 9

Program -190] Sorting Method Insertion Sort.

```
#include<stdio.h>
#include<conio.h>
void main()
{
int x[100], no,temp, i, d, k;
clrscr();
printf("\nEnter number of elements:");
scanf("%d", &no);
printf("\nEnter %d integers\n", no);
```

```
for ( i = 0 ; i < no ; i++ )
scanf("%d", &x[i]);
for ( i = 1 ; i <= no - 1 ; i++ )
{
for ( d = 0 ; d <= i - 1 ; d++ )
{
if ( x[i] < x[d] )
{
temp = x[d];
x[d] = x[i];
for ( k = i ; k > d ; k-- )
x[k] = x[k-1];
x[k+1] = temp;
}
}
}
printf("\nSorted list in ascending order:\n");
for ( i = 0 ; i < no ; i++ )
printf("%d\n", x[i]);
getch();
}
```

Input:

Enter number of elements:5

Enter 5 integers

4 5 8 9 6

Output:

Sorted list in ascending order:

4 5 6 8 9

Program -191] Sorting method Selection Sort.

```
#include<stdio.h>
#include<conio.h>
void main()
{
int x[100],temp, no, i, d;
clrscr();
printf("\nEnter number of elements:");
```

```
scanf("%d", &no);
printf("\nEnter %d integers\n", no);
for ( i = 0 ; i < no ; i++ )
scanf("%d", &x[i]);
for ( i = 0 ; i < ( no - 1) ; i++ )
{
for ( d = ( i + 1 ) ; d <= ( no - 1 ) ; d++ )
{
if ( x[i] > x[d] )
{
temp = x[i];
x[i] = x[d];
x[d] = temp;
}
}
}
printf("\nSorted list in ascending order:\n");
for ( i = 0 ; i < no ; i++ )
printf("%d\n", x[i]);
getch();
}
```

Input:

Enter number of elements:5

Enter 5 integers

4 5 8 9 6

Output:

Sorted list in ascending order:

4 5 6 8 9

Program -192] Get number's find even, odd & sum of them.

```
#include<stdio.h>
#include<conio.h>
void main()
{
int i,arr[10],evensum=0,oddsum=0,n;
clrscr();
printf("\nEnter number of elements:");
```

```
scanf("%d", &n);
printf("\nEnter %d integers\n", n);
for(i=0;i<n;i++)
scanf("%d",&arr[i]);
for(i=0;i<n;i++)
{
if(arr[i]%2==0)
{
printf("\n%d is even",arr[i]);
evensum=evensum+arr[i];
}
else
{
printf("\n%d is odd",arr[i]);
oddsum=oddsum+arr[i];
}
}
printf("\n\nThe sum of even element is:%d",evensum);
printf("\nThe sum of odd element is:%d",oddsum);
getch();
}
```

Input:

Enter number of elements:5

Enter 5 integers

1 2 3 4 5

Output:

1 is odd

2 is even

3 is odd

4 is even

5 is odd

The sum of even element is:6

The sum of odd element is:9

Program -193] Copy one array into another array in the reverse order.

```
#include<stdio.h>
#include<conio.h>
```

```
void main()
{
int arr1[10],arr2[10],i,j;
clrscr();
printf("\nEntre ten elements of array:");
for(i=0;i<=9;i++)
scanf("%d",&arr1[i]);
for(i=0,j=9;i<=9;i++,j--)
arr2[j]=arr1[i];
printf("\nElements in reversed order :");
for(j=0;j<=9;j++)
printf("%4d",arr2[j]);
getch();
}
```

Input:

Entre the five elements of first array:1 2 3 4 5 6 7 8 9 10

Output:

Elements in revers order into second array:10 9 8 7 6 5 4 3 2 1

Program -194] Program to computation of standard deviation.

```
#include<stdio.h>
#include<conio.h>
#include<math.h>
void main()
{
int da[11]={12,-8,11,6,7,-6,2,-9,2,11,14};
float sd[10],me=0;
int i,n=10;
clrscr();
for(i=0;i<=10;i++)
printf("%4d",da[i]);
for(i=0;i<=10;i++)
{
me=me+da[i];
}
me=me/n;
for(i=0;i<=10;i++)
```

```
sd[i]=sqrt(pow((da[i]-me),2))/n;
printf("\nMean:%f",me);
for(i=0;i<=10;i++)
{
printf("\nStandard Deviation of %d = %2f",da[i],sd[i]);
}
getch();
}
```

Output:

```
Mean:3.818182
Standard Deviation of 12 = 0.743802
Standard Deviation of -8 = 1.074380
Standard Deviation of 11 = 0.652893
Standard Deviation of 6 = 0.198347
Standard Deviation of 7 = .289256
Standard Deviation of -6 = 0.892562
Standard Deviation of 2 = 0.165289
Standard Deviation of -9 = 1.165289
Standard Deviation of 2 = 0.165289
Standard Deviation of 11 = 0.652853
Standard Deviation of 14 = 0.925620
```

Program -195] Program to calculation equation of straight line.

```
#include<stdio.h>
#include<conio.h>
#include<math.h>
void main()
{
int n=7,i,j;
float x[7]={7.0,7.5,8.5,8.0,9.0,9.5,10.0};
float y[7]={7.5,9.0,10.5,12.0,13.0,13.5,14.0};
float a,b;
float sx=0.0,sxy=0.0,sy=0.0,sxs=0.0;
float p1,p2,mx=0.0,my=0.0,yy;
clrscr();
for(i=0;i<=6;i++)
{
```

```
sx=sx+x[i];
sxy=sxy+x[i]*y[j];
sy=sy+y[i];
sxs=sxs+x[i]*x[i];
}
printf("\nSummation of X=%.2f",sx);
printf("\nSummation of XY=%.2f",sxy);
printf("\nSummation of Y=%.2f",sy);
printf("\nSummation of square of X=%.2f",sxs);
p1=(n*sxy-sx*sy);
p2=((n*sxs)-(sx*sx));
b=p1/p2;
printf("\n\np1 =%f",p1);
printf("\n\np2 =%f",p2);
printf("\n\nValue of b=%f",b);
mx=sx/n;
my=sy/n;
a=my-b*mx;
printf("\nValue of a=%f",a);
printf("\n\nEquation of the line is:Y=%.2f X %.2f",b,a);
getch();
}
```

Output:

```
Summation of X=59.50
Summation of XY=-16148.00
Summation of Y=79.50
Summation of square of X=512.75
p1 =-1130.00
p2 =49.00
Value of b=-23069.00
Value of a=196094.00
Equation of the line is: Y=-23069.00 X +196094.00
```

Program -196] Program to add bonus to employee salaries.

```
#include<stdio.h>
#include<conio.h>
void main()
```

```
{
void sal(int a[5]);
void net(int a[5], int b) ;
int a[5],i;
int b;
clrscr();
sal(a);
printf("\n Employee salaries:\n");
for(j=1;j<=5;j++)
printf("Employee%d -Rs %d\n",j,a[j]);
printf("\nEnter the bonus value:");
scanf("%d",&b);
net(a,b);
printf("\nRevised Salaries are:\n");
for(j=1;j<=5;j++)
printf("Employee%d -Rs %d\n",j,a[j]);
getch();
}
void sal(int a[5])
{
int j;
printf("\nEnter the salaries of employees:\n");
for(j=1;j<=5;j++)
{
printf("\nEmployee%d -Rs:",j+1);
scanf("%d",&a[j]);
}
}
void net(int a[5], int b)
{
int p;
for(p=1;p<=5;p++)
a[p]=a[p]+b;
}
```

Input:

Enter the salaries of 5 employees:

Employee1 -Rs:2000

Employee2 -Rs:3000

Employee3 -Rs:4000
Employee4 -Rs:5000
Employee5 -Rs:6000
Enter the bonus value:1000

Output:

Revised Salaries are:
Employee1 -Rs 3000
Employee2 -Rs 4000
Employee3 -Rs 5000
Employee4 -Rs 6000
Employee5 -Rs 7000

Program -197] Program binary to decimal conversion.

```
#include<stdio.h>
#include<conio.h>
void main()
{
double i;
int n,j,ans=0,x[10];
clrscr();
printf("How many digits in the binary no:");
scanf("%d",&n);
printf("\nEnter Binary Number:");
for(i=0;i<n;i++)
scanf("%ld",&x[i]);
i=0;
for(j=n-1;j>=0;j--)
{
ans+=x[j]*(double)pow(2,i);
i++;
}
printf("\nThe decimal equivalent is:%d",ans);
getch();
}
```

Input:

How many digits in the binary no:3
Enter Binary Number:1 1 1

Output:

The decimal equivalent is:7

Program -198] Program to decimal to binary conversion.

```
#include<stdio.h>
#include<conio.h>
void main()
{
int n,i,k=0,rem,x[10];
clrscr();
printf("Enter the decimal number:");
scanf("%d",&n);
while(n!=1)
{
rem=n%2;
x[k]=rem;
n=n/2;
k++;
}
x[k]=1;
printf("\nThe binary equivalent is:");
for(i=k;i>=0;i--)
printf(" %d",x[i]);
getch();
}
```

Input:

Enter the decimal number:8

Output:

The binary equivalent is: 1 0 0 0

Program -199] Program to perform operation union of two arrays.

```
#include<stdio.h>
#include<conio.h>
void main()
{
int i,k=0,a[15],b[15],c[30],j,n,n1;
```

```
clrscr();
printf("Enter number of elements for first array :");
scanf("%d",&n);
printf("Enter elemets of first array:");
for(i=0;i<n;i++)
scanf("%d",&a[i]);
printf("Enter number of elements for second array :");
scanf("%d",&n1);
printf("Enter elemets of second array:");
for(i=0;i<n1;i++)
scanf("%d",&b[i]);
for(i=0;i<n;i++)
{
c[k]=a[i];
k++;
}
for(i=0;i<n;i++)
{
for(j=0;j<n1;j++)
{
if(b[i]==a[j])
break;
}
if(j==n)
{
c[k]=b[i];
k++;
}
}
printf("\nThe union of array is:{");
for(i=0;i<k;i++)
printf(" %d",c[i]);
printf("}");
getch();
}
```

Input:

Enter number of elements for first array :3

Enter elemets of first array:4 5 6

Enter number of elements for second array :3
Enter elemets of second array:7 8 9
Output:
The union of array is:{ 4 5 6 7 8 9}

Program -200] Program to read two arrays and sort them and merge them to from
a third sorted array.

```
#include<stdio.h>
#include<conio.h>
void main()
{
int i,j,k,a[10],b[10],z[20],n,n1,temp;
clrscr();
printf("How many elements for ARRAY1 do you want:");
scanf("%d",&n);
printf("Enter the elemets of first array:\n");
for(i=0;i<n;i++)
scanf("%d",&a[i]);
for(i=0;i<n-1;i++)
for(j=i+1;j<n;j++)
{
if(a[i]>a[j])
{
temp=a[i];
a[i]=a[j];
a[j]=temp;
}
}
printf("How many elements for ARRAY2 do you want:");
scanf("%d",&n1);
printf("Enter the elemets of second array:\n");
for(i=0;i<n1;i++)
scanf("%d",&b[i]);
for(i=0;i<n1-1;i++)
for(j=i+1;j<n1;j++)
{
```

```
if(b[i]>b[j])
{
temp=b[i];
b[i]=b[j];
b[j]=temp;
}
}
i=0;j=0;k=0;
while(i<n && j<n1)
{
if(a[i]<=b[j])
{
z[k]=a[i];
i++;
k++;
}
if(a[i]>b[j])
{
z[k]=b[j];
k++;
j++;
}
}
while(i!=n)
{
z[k]=a[i];
i++;
k++;
}
while(j!=n1)
{
z[k]=b[j];
j++;
k++;
}
printf("\nThe Resultant Third Array is:");
for(i=0;i<k;i++)
printf(" %d",z[i]);
```

```
getch();
}
```

Input:

How many elements for ARRAY1 do you want:5
Enter the elemets of first array:
4 8 9 5 6
How many elements for ARRAY2 do you want:3
Enter the elemets of second array:
7 2 1

Output:

The Resultant Third Array is: 1 2 4 5 6 7 8 9

Program -201] Program to perform Intersection of two arrays.

```
#include<stdio.h>
#include<conio.h>
void main()
{
int i,k=0,a[10],b[10],r[20],j,n,n1;
clrscr();
printf("How many elements ARRAY-1:");
scanf("%d",&n);
printf("Enter the elemets of first array:");
for(i=0;i<n;i++)
scanf("%d",&a[i]);
printf("How many elements ARRAY-2:");
scanf("%d",&n1);
printf("Enter the elemets of second ARRAY-2:");
for(i=0;i<n1;i++)
scanf("%d",&b[i]);
for(j=0;j<n;j++)
{
for(i=0;i<n1;i++)
{
if(b[i]==a[j])
break;
}
if(i!=n1)
```

```
{
r[k]=b[i];
k++;
}
}
printf("\nThe intersection of array is is:{");
for(i=0;i<k;i++)
printf(" %d",r[i]);
printf("}");
getch();
}
```

Input:

How many elements ARRAY-1:3
Enter the elemets of first ARRAY:4 5 6
How many elements ARRAY-2:3
Enter the elemets of second ARRAY:5 6 7

Output:

The intersection of array is:{ 5 6}

CHAPTER THIRTEEN

Matrix Programs - Two Dimension Array

Program -202] Print the matrix(two dimensional array)

```
#include<stdio.h>
#include<conio.h>
main()
{
int i,j,mat[5][5],r,c;
clrscr();
printf("Enter Row:");
scanf("%d",&r);
printf("Enter Column:");
scanf("%d",&c);
printf("\nEnter the %dx%d matrix element:\n",r,c);
for(i=0;i<r;i++)
for(j=0;j<c;j++)
scanf("%d",&mat[i][j]);
printf("\nThe Given matrix is:\n");
for(i=0;i<r;i++)
{
for(j=0;j<c;j++)
{
printf("%d ",mat[i][j]);
}
printf("\n");
}
getch();
return(0);
```

```
}
```

Input:

Enter Row:3

Enter Column:3

Enter the 3x3 matrix element:

1 2 3 4 5 6 7 8 9

Output:

The Given matrix is:

1 2 3

4 5 6

7 8 9

Program -203] Search number from matrix.

```
#include<stdio.h>
#include<conio.h>
void main()
{
int i,j,mat[5][5],r,c,num,cnt=0;
clrscr();
printf("Enter Row:");
scanf("%d",&r);
printf("Enter Column:");
scanf("%d",&c);
printf("\nEnter the %dx%d matrix element:\n",r,c);
for(i=0;i<r;i++)
for(j=0;j<c;j++)
scanf("%d",&mat[i][j]);
printf("\nEnter the number do you want to search:");
scanf("%d",&num);
for(i=0;i<r;i++)
{
for(j=0;j<c;j++)
{
if(num==mat[i][j])
cnt++;
}
}
```

```
if(cnt==0)
printf("\nThe given number is not found in matrix");
else
printf("\nThe given number is found in %d times",cnt);
getch();
}
```

Input:

Enter Row:3

Enter Column:3

Enter the 3x3 matrix element:

1 2 3

4 5 6

7 8 9

Enter the number do you want to search:5

Output:

The given number is found in 1 times

Program -204] Program to perform operation addition of two matrices.

```
#include<stdio.h>
#include<conio.h>
main()
{
int a[3][3],b[3][3],c[3][3],i,j;
clrscr();
printf("\nEnter elements of first 3*3 matrix:\n\n");
for(i=0;i<3;i++)
for(j=0;j<3;j++)
scanf("%d",&a[i][j]);
printf("\nEnter elements of second 3*3 matrix:\n\n");
for(i=0;i<3;i++)
for(j=0;j<3;j++)
scanf("%d",&b[i][j]);
printf("\nAddition of two matrices:\n");
for(i=0;i<3;i++)
{
for(j=0;j<3;j++)
{
```

```
c[i][j]=a[i][j]+b[i][j];
printf("%d\t",c[i][j]);
}
printf("\n");
}
getch();
return(0);
}
```

Input:

Enter elements of first 3*3 matrix:

1 2 3

4 5 6

7 8 9

Enter elements of second 3*3 matrix:

1 2 3

4 5 6

7 8 9

Output:

Addition of two matrices:

2 4 6

8 10 12

14 16 18

Program -205] Program to search minimum no from two dimentional array.

```
#include<stdio.h>
#include<conio.h>
main()
{
int i,j,num[3][3],min=0;
clrscr();
printf("Enter the 3*3 matrix:\n");
for(i=0;i<3;i++)
for(j=0;j<3;j++)
scanf("%d",&num[i][j]);
min=num[0][0];
for(i=0;i<3;i++)
```

```
{
for(j=0;j<3;j++)
{
if(num[i][j]<min)
min=num[i][j];
}
}
printf("\nThe minimum no from given array is %d",min);
getch();
return(0);
}
```

Input:

Enter the 3*3 matrix:

7 8 9

4 5 6

1 2 3

Output:

The minimum no from given array is 1

Program -206] Program to find the largest element from 2*2 matrix.

```
#include<stdio.h>
#include<conio.h>
main()
{
static int a[2][2]={{5,10},{20,7}};
int i,j,big;
clrscr();
big=a[0][0];
printf("\n The matrix is:\n");
for(i=0;i<=1;i++)
{
for(j=0;j<=1;j++)
{
printf("%d\t",a[i][j]);
if(a[i][j]>big)
big=a[i][j];
}
```

```
printf("\n");
}
printf("\n Largest no in matrix is %d", big);
getch();
return(0);
}
```

Output:

The matrix is:

5 10

20 7

Largest no in matrix is 20

Program -207] Program to sort two dimentional array.

```
#include<stdio.h>
#include<conio.h>
main()
{
int a[3][3],b[9],i,j,k=0,temp;
clrscr();
printf("\nEnter 3*3 matrix:\n");
for(i=0;i<3;i++)
{
for(j=0;j<3;j++)
{
scanf("%d",&a[i][j]);
b[k]=a[i][j];
k++;
}
}
/*Sorting*/
for(i=0;i<9;i++)
{
for(j=i+1;j<9;j++)
{
if(b[i]>b[j])
{
temp = b[i];
```

```
b[i] = b[j];
b[j] = temp;
}
}
}
k=0;
printf("\n Sorted matrix is:\n");
for(i=0;i<3;i++)
{
for(j=0;j<3;j++)
{
a[i][j]=b[k];
printf("%5d",a[i][j]);
k++;
}
printf("\n");
}
getch();
return(0);
}
```

Input:

Enter 3*3 matrix:

4 5 6

8 9 7

2 3 1

Output:

Sorted matrix is:

1 2 3

4 5 6

7 8 9

Program -208] Program to print even no from two dimentional array.

```
#include<stdio.h>
#include<conio.h>
void main()
{
int i,j,mat[5][5],r,c;
```

```
clrscr();
printf("Enter Row:");
scanf("%d",&r);
printf("Enter Column:");
scanf("%d",&c);
printf("\nEnter the %dx%d matrix element:\n",r,c);
for(i=0;i<r;i++)
for(j=0;j<c;j++)
scanf("%d",&mat[i][j]);
printf("\nEven Number:");
for(i=0;i<r;i++)
{
for(j=0;j<c;j++)
{
if(mat[i][j]%2==0)
printf("\n%d",mat[i][j]);
}
}
getch();
}
```

Input:

Enter Row:3
Enter Column:3
Enter the 3x3 matrix element:
4 5 6
8 9 7
2 1 3

Output:

Even Number:
4 6 8 2

Program -209] Program to print Odd no from two dimentional array.

```
#include<stdio.h>
#include<conio.h>
void main()
{
int i,j,mat[5][5],r,c;
```

```
clrscr();
printf("Enter Row:");
scanf("%d",&r);
printf("Enter Column:");
scanf("%d",&c);
printf("\nEnter the %dx%d matrix element:\n",r,c);
for(i=0;i<r;i++)
for(j=0;j<c;j++)
scanf("%d",&mat[i][j]);
printf("\nOdd Number:");
for(i=0;i<r;i++)
{
for(j=0;j<c;j++)
{
if(mat[i][j]%2!=0)
printf("\n%d",mat[i][j]);
}
}
getch();
}
```

Input:

```
Enter Row:3
Enter Column:3
Enter the 3x3 matrix element:
1 2 3
4 5 6
7 8 9
```

Output:

```
Odd Number:
1 3 5 7 9
```

Program -210] Program to print Prime no from two dimentional array.

```
#include<stdio.h>
#include<conio.h>
void main()
{
int i,j,k,mat[5][5],r,c,fact=0;
```

```
clrscr();
printf("Enter Row:");
scanf("%d",&r);
printf("Enter Column:");
scanf("%d",&c);
printf("\nEnter the %dx%d matrix element:\n",r,c);
for(i=0;i<r;i++)
for(j=0;j<c;j++)
scanf("%d",&mat[i][j]);
printf("\nPrime Number:");
for(i=0;i<r;i++)
{
for(j=0;j<c;j++)
{
fact=0;
for(k=1;k<=mat[i][j];k++)
{
if(mat[i][j]%k==0)
fact++;
}
if(fact==2)
printf("\t%d",mat[i][j]);
}
}
getch();
}
```

Input:

Enter Row:3
Enter Column:3
Enter the 3x3 matrix element:
7 8 9
5 4 6
2 1 3

Output:

Prime Number:7 5 2 3

Program -211] Program to perform Matrix Multiplication.

```
#include<stdio.h>
#include<conio.h>
main()
{
int m, n, p, q, c, d, k, sum = 0;
int first[10][10], second[10][10], mul[10][10];
clrscr();
printf("\nFirst Matrix:\n");
printf("\nEnter the number of rows:");
scanf("%d",&m);
printf("Enter the number of columns:");
scanf("%d",&n);
printf("\nEnter the elements of first %d*%d matrix\n",m,n);
for ( c = 0 ; c < m ; c++ )
for ( d = 0 ; d < n ; d++ )
scanf("%d",&first[c][d]);
printf("\nSecond Matrix:\n");
printf("\nEnter the number of rows:");
scanf("%d",&p);
printf("Enter the number of columns:");
scanf("%d",&q);
if ( n != p )
printf("\nMatrices with entered orders can't be multiplied with each other.\n");
else
{
printf("\nEnter the elements of second %d*%d matrix\n",p,q);
for ( c = 0 ; c < p ; c++ )
for ( d = 0 ; d < q ; d++ )
scanf("%d",&second[c][d]);
for ( c = 0 ; c < m ; c++ )
{
for ( d = 0 ; d < n ; d++ )
{
for ( k = 0 ; k < p ; k++ )
{
sum = sum + first[c][k]*second[k][d];
}
```

```
mul[c][d] = sum;
sum = 0;
}
}
printf("\nProduct of entered matrices:-\n");
for ( c = 0 ; c < m ; c++ )
{
for ( d = 0 ; d < q ; d++ )
printf("%d\t",mul[c][d]);
printf("\n");
}
}
getch();
return 0;
}
```

Input:

First Matrix:

Enter the number of rows:3

Enter the number of columns:3

Enter the elements of first 3*3 matrix

1 2 3

4 5 6

7 8 9

Second Matrix:

Enter the number of rows:3

Enter the number of columns:3

Enter the elements of second 3*3 matrix

1 2 3

1 2 3

1 2 3

Output:

Product of entered matrices:-

6 12 18

15 30 45

24 48 72

Program -212] Transpose Of matrix

```
#include<stdio.h>
#include<conio.h>
void main()
{
int m, n, c, d, matrix[10][10], transpose[10][10];
clrscr();
printf("\nEnter the number of rows:");
scanf("%d",&m);
printf("Enter the number of columns:");
scanf("%d",&n);
printf("\nEnter the elements of %d*%dmatrix \n",m,n);
for( c = 0 ; c < m ; c++ )
{
for( d = 0 ; d < n ; d++ )
{
scanf("%d",&matrix[c][d]);
}
}
for( c = 0 ; c < m ; c++ )
{
for( d = 0 ; d < n ; d++ )
{
transpose[d][c] = matrix[c][d];
}
}
printf("Transpose of entered matrix :-\n");
for( c = 0 ; c < n ; c++ )
{
for( d = 0 ; d < m ; d++ )
{
printf("%d\t",transpose[c][d]);
}
printf("\n");
}
getch();
}
```

Input:

Enter the number of rows:3

Enter the number of columns:3
Enter the elements of 3*3matrix
7 8 9
4 5 6
1 2 3

Output:

Transpose of entered matrix :-
7 4 1
8 5 2
9 6 3

Program -213] Program to print the upper triangular matrix.

```
#include<stdio.h>
#include<conio.h>
main()
{
int a[3][3],i,j;
clrscr();
printf("\n Upper triangular 3*3 matrix is as follows:\n");
for(i=0;i<3;i++)
{
for(j=0;j<3;j++)
{
if(i<=j)
a[i][j]=1;
else
a[i][j]=0;
printf("%d\t",a[i][j]);
}
printf("\n");
}
getch();
return(0);
}
```

Output:

Upper triangular 3*3 matrix is as follows:
1 1 1

0 1 1
0 0 1

Program -214] Program to calculate sum of upper triangular matrix.

```
#include<stdio.h>
#include<conio.h>
void main()
{
int sum=0,i,j,a[3][3];
clrscr();
printf("\nEnter the 3*3 matrix:\n");
for(i=0;i<3;i++)
for(j=0;j<3;j++)
scanf("%4d",&a[i][j]);
printf("\nGiven matrix is\n");
for(i=0;i<3;i++)
{
for(j=0;j<3;j++)
printf("%4d",a[i][j]);
printf("\n");
}
for(i=0;i<3;i++)
{
for(j=0;j<3;j++)
{
if(j>=i)
sum+=a[i][j];
}
}
printf("\nSum of upper triangular matrix is:%d",sum);
getch();
}
```

Input:

Enter the 3*3 matrix:

1 2 3
0 2 3
0 0 3

Given matrix is
1 2 3
0 2 3
0 0 3
Output:
Sum of upper triangular matrix is:14

Program -215] Program to find out minimum number from upper triangular matrix.

```
#include<stdio.h>
#include<conio.h>
void main()
{
int i,j,mat[5][5],r,c;
clrscr();
printf("\nEnter Row:");
scanf("%d",&r);
printf("\nEnter Column:");
scanf("%d",&c);
printf("\nEnter the %dx%d matrix element:\n",r,c);
for(i=0;i<r;i++)
for(j=0;j<c;j++)
scanf("%d",&mat[i][j]);
for(i=0;i<r;i++)
{
for(j=0;j<c;j++)
{
if(mat[i][j]<mat[i+1][j+1])
mat[i+1][j+1]=mat[i][j];
}
}
printf("\n The minimum number of upper triangular matrix is:%d",mat[i][j]);
getch();
}
```

Input:

Enter Row:3
Enter Column:3
Enter the 3x3 matrix element:
6 8 9
0 7 8
0 0 1

Output:

The minimum number of triangular matrix is:1

Program -216] Program to find out maximum number from upper triangular matrix.

```
#include<stdio.h>
#include<conio.h>
void main()
{
int i,j,mat[5][5],r,c,big;
clrscr();
printf("\nEnter Row:");
scanf("%d",&r);
printf("\nEnter Column:");
scanf("%d",&c);
printf("\nEnter the %dx%d matrix element:\n",r,c);
for(i=0;i<r;i++)
for(j=0;j<c;j++)
scanf("%d",&mat[i][j]);
big=mat[0][0];
for(i=0;i<r;i++)
{
for(j=0;j<c;j++)
{
if(j>=i)
{
if(mat[i][j]>big)
big=mat[i][j];
}
}
```

```
}
printf("\n The maximum number of upper triangular matrix is:%d",big);
getch();
}
```

Input:

Enter Row:3

Enter Column:3

Enter the 3x3 matrix element:

1 2 3

0 0 6

8 0 1

Output:

The maximum number of upper triangular matrix is:6

Program -217] Program to generate lower triangular matrix.

```
#include<stdio.h>
#include<conio.h>
void main()
{
int i,j,a[3][3];
clrscr();
printf("\n Lower Triangular Martix \n");
for(i=0;i<3;i++)
{
for(j=0;j<3;j++)
{
if(i>=j)
a[i][j]=1;
else
a[i][j]=0;
printf("%d\t",a[i][j]);
}
printf("\n");
}
getch();
}
```

Output:

```
Lower Triangular Martix
1 0 0
1 1 0
1 1 1
```

Program -218] Program to print minimum number from lower triagular matrix.

```
#include<stdio.h>
#include<conio.h>
void main()
{
int i,j,mat[5][5],r,c;
clrscr();
printf("Enter Row:");
scanf("%d",&r);
printf("\nEnter Column:");
scanf("%d",&c);
printf("\nEnter the %dx%d matrix element:\n",r,c);
for(i=0;i<r;i++)
for(j=0;j<c;j++)
scanf("%d",&mat[i][j]);
printf("\nLower Triangular Martix \n");
for(i=0;i<r;i++)
{
for(j=0;j<c;j++)
{
if(i<j)
mat[i][j]=0;
else
mat[i][j]=mat[i][j];
printf("%d\t",mat[i][j]);
}
printf("\n");
}
for(i=0;i<r;i++)
{
for(j=0;j<c;j++)
```

```
{
if(mat[i][j]<mat[i+1][j+1])
mat[i+1][j+1]=mat[i][j];
}
}
printf("\n The minimum number of lower triangular matrix is:%d",mat[i][j]);
getch();
}
```

Input:

Enter Row:3
Enter Column:3
Enter the 3x3 matrix element:
1 2 3
4 5 6
7 8 9
Lower Triangular Martix
1 0 0
4 5 0
7 8 9

Output:

The minimum number of lower triangular matrix is:1

Program -219] Program to print maximum number from lower triagular matrix.

```
#include<stdio.h>
#include<conio.h>
void main()
{
int i,j,mat[5][5],r,c,big=0;
clrscr();
printf("Enter Row:");
scanf("%d",&r);
printf("Enter Column:");
scanf("%d",&c);
printf("\nEnter the %dx%d matrix element:\n",r,c);
for(i=0;i<r;i++)
```

```
for(j=0;j<c;j++)
scanf("%d",&mat[i][j]);
printf("\n Lower Triangular Martix \n");
for(i=0;i<r;i++)
{
for(j=0;j<c;j++)
{
if(i<j)
mat[i][j]=0;
else
mat[i][j]=mat[i][j];
printf("%d\t",mat[i][j]);
}
printf("\n");
}
big=mat[0][0];
for(i=0;i<r;i++)
{
for(j=0;j<c;j++)
{
if(j>=i)
{
if(mat[i][j]>big)
big=mat[i][j];
}
}
}
printf("\n The maximum number of triangular matrix is:%d",big);
getch();
}
```

Input:

Enter Row:3
Enter Column:3
Enter the 3x3 matrix element:
4 5 6
8 2 9
4 6 8
Lower Triangular Martix

4 0 0
8 2 0
4 6 8

Output:

The maximum number of lower triangular matrix is:8

Program -220] Program to print sum of lower triagular matrix.

```
#include<stdio.h>
#include<conio.h>
void main()
{
int i,j,mat[5][5],r,c,sum=0;
clrscr();
printf("Enter Row:");
scanf("%d",&r);
printf("Enter Column:");
scanf("%d",&c);
printf("\nEnter the %dx%d matrix element:\n",r,c);
for(i=0;i<r;i++)
for(j=0;j<c;j++)
scanf("%d",&mat[i][j]);
printf("\n Lower Triangular Martix \n");
for(i=0;i<r;i++)
{
for(j=0;j<c;j++)
{
if(i<j)
mat[i][j]=0;
else
{
mat[i][j]=mat[i][j];
sum=sum+mat[i][j];
}
printf("%d\t",mat[i][j]);
}
printf("\n");
}
```

```
printf("\n The total sum of lower triangular matrix is:%d",sum);
getch();
}
```

Input:

Enter Row:3
Enter Column:3
Enter the 3x3 matrix element:
7 8 9
5 4 6
2 1 3

Output:

Lower Triangular Martix
7 0 0
5 4 0
2 1 3
The total sum of lower triangular matrix is:22

Program -221] Program to print the identity matrix.

```
#include<stdio.h>
#include<conio.h>
main()
{
int a[3][3],i,j;
clrscr();
printf("\nIdentity matrix is as follows:\n\n");
for(i=0;i<3;i++)
{
for(j=0;j<3;j++)
{
if(i==j)
a[i][j]=1;
else
a[i][j]=0;
printf("%d\t",a[i][j]);
}
printf("\n");
}
```

```
getch();
return(0);
}
```

Output:

Identity matrix is as follows:

```
1 0 0
0 1 0
0 0 1
```

Program 222] Program to calculate and print sum of row elements.

```
#include<stdio.h>
#include<conio.h>
main()
{
int a[3][3],i,j,sum;
clrscr();
printf("\n Enter 3*3 matrix:\n\n");
for(i=0;i<3;i++)
for(j=0;j<3;j++)
scanf("%d",&a[i][j]);
for(i=0;i<3;i++)
{
sum=0;
for(j=0;j<3;j++)
{
printf("%d\t",a[i][j]);
sum +=a[i][j];
}
printf("Sum=%d",sum);
printf("\n");
}
getch();
return(0);
}
```

Input:

Enter 3*3 matrix:

5 4 8

7 9 6
2 1 3

Output:

5 4 8 Sum=17
7 9 6 Sum=22
2 1 3 Sum=6

Program -223] Program to calculate and print sum of column elements.

```
#include<stdio.h>
#include<conio.h>
main()
{
int a[3][3],i,j,sum[3];
clrscr();
printf("\nEnter 3*3 matrix:\n\n");
for(i=0;i<3;i++)
for(j=0;j<3;j++)
scanf("%d",&a[i][j]);
for(i=0;i<3;i++)
{
sum[i]=0;
for(j=0;j<3;j++)
{
printf("%d\t", a[i][j]);
sum[i] +=a[j][i];
}
printf("Column Sum=%d",sum[i]);
printf("\n");
}
getch();
return(0);
}
```

Input:

Enter 3*3 matrix:

7 8 9
6 5 4
2 1 3

Output:

7 8 9 Column Sum=15
6 5 4 Column Sum=14
2 1 3 Column Sum=16

Program -224] Program to print sum of row and column of matrix.

```
#include<stdio.h>
#include<conio.h>
void main()
{
int i,j,k,mat[5][5],r,c,rowsum=0,colsum=0;
clrscr();
printf("Enter Row:");
scanf("%d",&r);
printf("Enter Column:");
scanf("%d",&c);
printf("\nEnter the %dx%d matrix element:\n",r,c);
for(i=0;i<r;i++)
for(j=0;j<c;j++)
scanf("%d",&mat[i][j]);
rintf("\n The sum of Row and Column of given Martix is: \n\n");
for(i=0;i<r;i++)
{
for(j=0;j<c;j++)
{
printf("\t%d",mat[i][j]);
rowsum=rowsum+mat[i][j];
if(j==c-1)
printf("|");
}
printf("%4d",rowsum);
rowsum=0;
printf("\n");
}
for(k=0;k<c;k++)
printf("\t--");
printf("\n");
```

```
for(j=0;j<c;j++)
{
for(i=0;i<r;i++)
{
colsum=colsum+mat[i][j];
}
printf("\t%d",colsum);
colsum=0;
}
getch();
}
```

Input:

Enter Row:3

Enter Column:3

Enter the 3x3 matrix element:

1 2 3

4 5 6

7 8 9

Output:

The sum of Row and Column of given Martix is:

1 2 3| 6

4 5 6| 15

7 8 9| 24

-- -- --

12 15 18

Program -225] Program to find max number from row of matrix.

```
#include<stdio.h>
#include<conio.h>
void main()
{
int i,j,k,mat[5][5],r,c,max;
clrscr();
printf("Enter Row:");
scanf("%d",&r);
printf("Enter Column:");
scanf("%d",&c);
```

```
printf("\nEnter the %dx%d matrix element:\n",r,c);
for(i=0;i<r;i++)
for(j=0;j<c;j++)
scanf("%d",&mat[i][j]);
printf("\n The max number from Row of given Martix is: \n\n");
for(i=0;i<r;i++)
{
max=mat[i][0];
for(j=0;j<c;j++)
{
if(mat[i][j]>max)
max=mat[i][j];
printf("\t%d",mat[i][j]);
if(j==c-1)
printf("|");
}
printf("%4d",max);
printf("\n");
}
getch();
}
```

Input:

Enter Row:3

Enter Column:3

Enter the 3x3 matrix element:

8 4 5

7 9 6

2 1 3

Output:

The max number from Row of given Martix is:

8 4 5| 8

7 9 6| 9

2 1 3| 3

Program -226] Program to find max numbrer from column of matrix.

```
#include<stdio.h>
#include<conio.h>
```

```
void main()
{
int i,j,k,mat[5][5],r,c,max;
clrscr();
printf("Enter Row:");
scanf("%d",&r);
printf("Enter Column:");
scanf("%d",&c);
printf("\nEnter the %dx%d matrix element:\n",r,c);
for(i=0;i<r;i++)
for(j=0;j<c;j++)
scanf("%d",&mat[i][j]);
printf("\n The max number from Column of given Martix is: \n");
for(i=0;i<r;i++)
{
for(j=0;j<c;j++)
{
printf("\t%d",mat[i][j]);
}
printf("\n");
}
for(k=0;k<c;k++)
printf("\t--");
printf("\n");
for(j=0;j<c;j++)
{
max=mat[0][j];
for(i=0;i<r;i++)
{
if(mat[i][j]>max)
max=mat[i][j];
}
printf("\t%d",max);
}
getch();
}
```

Input:

Enter Row:3

Enter Column:3
Enter the 3x3 matrix element:
5 4 6
8 9 7
2 1 3

Output:

The max number from Column of given Martix is:
5 4 6
8 9 7
2 1 3
-- -- --
8 9 7

Program -227] Program to find minimum number from row of matrix

```
#include<stdio.h>
#include<conio.h>
void main()
{
int i,j,k,mat[5][5],r,c,min;
clrscr();
printf("Enter Row:");
scanf("%d",&r);
printf("Enter Column:");
scanf("%d",&c);
printf("\nEnter the %dx%d matrix element:\n",r,c);
for(i=0;i<r;i++)
for(j=0;j<c;j++)
scanf("%d",&mat[i][j]);
printf("\n The min number from Row of given Martix is: \n\n");
for(i=0;i<r;i++)
{
min=mat[i][0];
for(j=0;j<c;j++)
{
if(mat[i][j]<min)
min=mat[i][j];
printf("\t%d",mat[i][j]);
```

```
if(j==c-1)
printf("|");
}
printf("%4d",min);
printf("\n");
}
getch();
}
```

Input:

Enter Row:3

Enter Column:3

Enter the 3x3 matrix element:

5 4 6

8 9 5

1 2 3

Output:

The min number from Row of given Martix is:

5 4 6| 4

8 9 5| 5

1 2 3| 1

Program -228] Program to find minimum number from column of matrix.

```
#include<stdio.h>
#include<conio.h>
void main()
{
int i,j,k,mat[5][5],r,c,min;
clrscr();
printf("Enter Row:");
scanf("%d",&r);
printf("Enter Column:");
scanf("%d",&c);
printf("\nEnter the %dx%d matrix element:\n",r,c);
for(i=0;i<r;i++)
for(j=0;j<c;j++)
scanf("%d",&mat[i][j]);
```

```
printf("\n The minimum number from Column of given Martix is: \n");
for(i=0;i<r;i++)
{
for(j=0;j<c;j++)
{
printf("\t%d",mat[i][j]);
}
printf("\n");
}
for(k=0;k<c;k++)
printf("\t--");
printf("\n");
for(j=0;j<c;j++)
{
min=mat[0][j];
for(i=0;i<r;i++)
{
if(mat[i][j]<min)
min=mat[i][j];
}
printf("\t%d",min);
}
getch();
}
```

Input:

```
Enter Row:3
Enter Column:3
Enter the 3x3 matrix element:
5 0 6
0 2 3
4 8 0
```

Output:

```
The minimum number from Column of given Martix is:
5 0 6
0 2 3
4 8 0
-- -- --
0 0 0
```

Program -229] Program to obtain determinant value of 3*3 matrix.

```
#include<stdio.h>
#include<conio.h>
#include<math.h>
main()
{
int x[10][10],i,j,a,sum,p;
clrscr();
printf("\nEnter 3*3 matrix:\n\n");
for(i=0;i<=2;i++)
{
for(j=0;j<=2;j++)
scanf("%d",&x[i][j]);
}
sum=0;
j=1;
a=2;
for(i=0;i<=2;i++)
{
p=pow(-1,i);
if(i==2)
a=1;
sum=sum+(x[0][i]*(x[1][j]*x[2][a]-x[2][j]*x[1][a]))*p;
j=0;
}
printf("\nDeterminant of the given matrix is %d",sum);
getch();
return(0);
}
```

Input:

Enter 3*3 matrix:

4 8 9

0 5 6

3 0 2

Output:

Determinant of the given matrix is 49

Program -230] Program to Check whether square matrix is symmetric or not.

```
#include<stdio.h>
#include<conio.h>
void main()
{
int mat[3][3],i,j,cnt=0;
clrscr();
printf("\nEnter the 3*3 matrix:\n\n");
for(i=0;i<3;i++)
for(j=0;j<3;j++)
scanf("%d",&mat[i][j]);
for(i=0;i<3;i++)
{
for(j=i;j<3;j++)
{
if(mat[i][j]==mat[j][i])
cnt++;
}
}
if(cnt==6)
printf("\n\nThe given matrix is symmetric");
else
printf("\n\nThe given matrix is not symmetric");
getch();
}
```

Input:

Enter the 3*3 matrix:

1 1 1
1 1 1
1 1 1

Output:

The given matrix is symmetric

Program -231] Program to perform operaion matrix substraction.

```
#include<stdio.h>
#include<conio.h>
main()
{
int m, n, c, d, first[10][10], second[10][10], difference[10][10];
clrscr();
printf("Enter the number of rows:");
scanf("%d",&m);
printf("\nEnter the number of columns:");
scanf("%d",&n);
printf("\nEnter the elements of first matrix\n");
for ( c = 0 ; c < m ; c++ )
for ( d = 0 ; d < n ; d++ )
scanf("%d",&first[c][d]);
printf("\nEnter the elements of second matrix\n");
for ( c = 0 ; c < m ; c++ )
for ( d = 0 ; d < n ; d++ )
scanf("%d",&second[c][d]);
for ( c = 0 ; c < m ; c++ )
for ( d = 0 ; d < n ; d++ )
difference[c][d] = first[c][d] - second[c][d];
printf("\nDifference of entered matrices:-\n");
for ( c = 0 ; c < m ; c++ )
{
for ( d = 0 ; d < n ; d++ )
printf("%d\t",difference[c][d]);
printf("\n");
}
getch();
return 0;
}
```

Input:

```
Enter the number of rows:3
Enter the number of columns:3
Enter the elements of first matrix
7 8 9
4 5 6
1 2 3
```

Enter the elements of second matrix

1 2 3

1 2 3

1 2 3

Output:

Difference of entered matrices:-

6 6 6

3 3 3

0 0 0

CHAPTER FOURTEEN

Pointer Programs

Program -232] Addition of two numbers using pointer.

```
#include<stdio.h>
#include<conio.h>
main()
{
int first, second, *p, *q, sum;
clrscr();
printf("Enter two integers numbers to add:");
scanf("%d%d", &first, &second);
p = &first;
q = &second;
sum = *p + *q;
printf("\nSum of entered numbers = %d\n",sum);
getch();
return 0;
}
```

Input:

Enter two integers numbers to add:89 56

Output:

Sum of entered numbers = 145

Program -233] Program to search string using pointer.

```
#include<stdio.h>
#include<conio.h>
int matstr(char*, char*);
main()
{
```

```
char str1[200],str2[200];
int pos;
clrscr();
printf("\nEnter some text:");
gets(str1);
printf("Enter a string to find\n");
gets(str2);
pos = matstr(str1,str2);
if(pos!=-1)
printf("Found at location %d\n", pos+1);
else
printf("Not found.\n");
getch();
return 0;
}
int matstr(char *a, char *b)
{
int c;
int pos = 0;
char *x, *y;
x = a;
y = b;
while(*a)
{
while(*x==*y)
{
x++;
y++;
if(*x=='\0'||*y=='\0')
break;
}
if(*y=='\0')
break;
a++;
pos++;
x = a;
y = b;
}
```

```
if(*a)
return pos;
else
return -1;
}
```

Input:

Enter some text:ACME IT Consulatancy & Services
Enter a string to find
IT

Output:

Found at location 6

Program -234] Perform operations sum,average and standerd deviation using function.

```
#include<stdio.h>
#include<conio.h>
#include<math.h>
void function(int*,int*,double*);
void main()
{
int sum,avg;
double stdev;
clrscr();
function(&sum,&avg,&stdev);
printf("\nSum=%d\nAverage=%d\nStanderd
deviation=%lf",sum,avg,stdev);
getch();
}
void function(int *sum,int *avg,double *stdev)
{
int n1,n2,n3,n4,n5;
printf("\n Enter 5 numbers:");
scanf("%d%d%d%d%d",&n1,&n2,&n3,&n4,&n5);
*sum=n1+n2+n3+n4+n5;
*avg=*sum/5;
*stdev=sqrt((pow((n1-*avg),2)+pow((n2-*avg),2)
```

```
+pow((n3-*avg),2)+pow((n4-*avg),2)+
pow((n5-*avg),2))/4);
}
```

Input:

Enter 5 numbers:

Number1:4

Number2:5

Number3:6

Number4:2

Number5:3

Output:

Sum=20

Average=4

Standerd deviation=1.581139

Program -235] Program of pointer to pointer.

```
#include<stdio.h>
#include<conio.h>
void main()
{
int a=7,*b,**c;
clrscr();
b=&a;
c=&b;
printf("\nAddress of i:%u",&a);
printf("\nAddress of j:%u",*c);
printf("\nAddress of k:%u",&c);
printf("\nValue of i:%d",*(&a));
printf("\nValue of j:%d",*b);
printf("\nValue of k:%d",**c);
getch();
}
```

Ouptput:

Address of i:65524

Address of j:65524

Address of k:65520

Value of i:3

Value of j:3
Value of k:3

CHAPTER FIFTEEN

String Programs

Program -236] Program calculate string length using strlen() function.

```
#include<stdio.h>
#include<conio.h>
#include<string.h>
main()
{
char str[200];
int length;
clrscr();
printf("Enter a string to calculate it's length\n");
gets(str);
length = strlen(str);
printf("\nLength of entered string is = %d\n",length);
getch();
return 0;
}
```

Input:

Enter a string to calculate it's length

ACME IT

Output:

Length of entered string is = 7

Program -237] Program calculate string length without using strlen() function.

```
#include<stdio.h>
#include<conio.h>
main()
```

```
{
char str[200], *pointer;
int length = 0;
clrscr();
printf("Enter a string:");
gets(str);
pointer = str;
while(*(pointer+length))
length++;
printf("\nLength of entered string = %d",length);
getch();
return 0;
}
```

Input:

Enter a string:ACME IT Consultancy & Services

Output:

Length of entered string = 30

Program -238] Compare Two Strings Using strcmp.

```
#include<stdio.h>
#include<conio.h>
#include<string.h>
main()
{
char str1[200], str2[200];
clrscr();
printf("\nEnter the first string:");
gets(str1);
printf("\nEnter the second string:");
gets(str2);
if( strcmp(str1,str2) == 0 )
printf("\nEntered strings are equal.");
else
printf("\nEntered strings are not equal.");
getch();
return 0;
}
```

Input:
Enter the first string:ACME
Enter the second string:ACME
Output:
Entered strings are equal.

Program -239] Compare Two Strings without using strcmp.

```
#include<stdio.h>
#include<conio.h>
void main()
{
char str1[10],str2[10];
int i;
clrscr();
printf("\nEnter first string:");
gets(str1);
printf("\nEnter second string:");
gets(str2);
i=compare(str1,str2);
if(i==0)
printf("\nStrings are equal");
else
printf("\nStrings are not equal");
getch();
}
int compare(char s1[], char s2[])
{
int cnt = 0;
while( s1[cnt] == s2[cnt] )
{
if( s1[cnt] == '\0' || s2[cnt] == '\0' )
break;
cnt++;
}
if( s1[cnt] == '\0' && s2[cnt] == '\0' )
return 0;
else
```

```
return 1;
}
```

Input:

Enter first string:ACME IT

Enter second string:ACME IT

Output:

Strings are equal

Program -240] Copy string using strcpy() function.

```
#include<stdio.h>
#include<conio.h>
#include<string.h>
main()
{
char sourcestr[] = "C program";
char destinationstr[50];
clrscr();
strcpy(destinationstr, sourcestr);
printf("Source string: %s\n", sourcestr);
printf("Destination string: %s\n", destinationstr);
getch();
return 0;
}
```

Output:

Source string: C program

Destination string: C program

Program -241] Program to concanate two strings using strcat() function.

```
#include<stdio.h>
#include<conio.h>
#include<string.h>
main()
{
char str1[100], str2[100];
clrscr();
printf("Enter the first string:");
```

```
gets(str1);
printf("Enter the second string:");
gets(str2);
strcat(str1,str2);
printf("String obtained on concatenation is %s\n",str1);
getch();
return 0;
}
```

Input:

Enter the first string:ACME

Enter the second string: IT

Output:

String obtained on concatenation is ACME IT

Program -242] Program to concanate two strings without using strcat() function.

```
#include<stdio.h>
#include<conio.h>
void concatstr(char*, char*);
main()
{
char str1[100], str2[100];
clrscr();
printf("Enter source string:");
gets(str1);
printf("\nEnter string to concatenate:");
gets(str2);
concatstr(str1, str2);
printf("String after concatenation is \"%s\"\n", str1);
getch();
return 0;
}
void concatstr(char *first, char *second)
{
while(*first)
first++;
while(*second)
```

```
{
*first = *second;
second++;
first++;
}
*first = '\0';
}
```

Input:

Enter source string:ACME IT

Enter string to concatenate: Consultancy & Services

Output:

String after concatenation is "ACME IT Consultancy & Services"

Program -243] Print reverse of given string.

```
#include<stdio.h>
#include<conio.h>
#include<string.h>
main()
{
char str[100];
clrscr();
printf("\nEnter a string :");
gets(str);
strrev(str);
printf("Reverse of entered string is \n%s\n",str);
getch();
return 0;
}
```

Input:

Enter a string to revers :EMCA

Output:

Reverse of entered string is

ACME

Program -244] Print string reverse using recursion.

```
#include<stdio.h>
```

```
#include<conio.h>
#include<string.h>
void rev(char*,int,int);
main()
{
char str[100];
clrscr();
printf("Enter string:");
gets(str);
rev(str, 0, strlen(str)-1);
printf("%s\n",str);
getch();
return 0;
}
void rev(char *x, int start, int stop)
{
char a, b, c;
if ( start >= stop )
return;
c = *(x+start);
*(x+start) = *(x+stop);
*(x+stop) = c;
rev(x, ++start, --stop);
}
```

Input:

Enter string:Good Day!!!

Output:

!!!yaD dooG

Program -245] Program to check whether string is palindrome or not.

```
#include<stdio.h>
#include<conio.h>
#include<string.h>
main()
{
char str1[100], str2[100];
clrscr();
```

```
printf("Enter the string to check if it is a palindrome:");
gets(str1);
strcpy(str2,str1);
strrev(str2);
if( strcmp(str1,str2) == 0 )
printf("Entered string is a palindrome.\n");
else
printf("Entered string is not a pailndrome.\n");
getch();
return 0;
}
```

Input:

Enter the string to check if it is a palindrome:MADAM

Output:

Entered string is a palindrome.

Program -246] Remove vowels from string.

```
#include<stdio.h>
#include<conio.h>
#include<stdlib.h>
#include<string.h>
#define TRUE 1
#define FALSE 0
int chkvowel(char);
main()
{
char str[100], *temp, *pointer, ch, *bgn;
clrscr();
printf("Enter a string:");
gets(str);
temp = str;
pointer = (char*)malloc(100);
if( pointer == NULL )
{
printf("Unable to allocate memory.\n");
exit(EXIT_FAILURE);
}
```

```
bgn = pointer;
while(*temp)
{
ch = *temp;
if ( !chkvowel(ch) )
{
*pointer = ch;
pointer++;
}
temp++;
}
*pointer = '\0';
pointer = bgn;
strcpy(str, pointer);
free(pointer);
printf("String after removing vowel is \"%s\"\n", str);
getch();
return 0;
}
int chkvowel(char a)
{
if ( a >= 'A' && a <= 'Z' )
a = a + 'a' - 'A';
if ( a == 'a' || a == 'e' || a == 'i' || a == 'o' || a == 'u')
return TRUE;
return FALSE;
}
```

Input:

Enter a string:MADAM

Output:

String after removing vowel is "MDM"

Program -247] Program to find substring of string.

```
#include<stdio.h>
#include<conio.h>
#include<malloc.h>
char* substr(char*, int, int);
```

```
main()
{
char str[100], *pointer;
int pos, len;
clrscr();
printf("Enter a string:");
gets(str);
printf("\nEnter the position and length of substring:");
scanf("%d%d",&pos, &len);
pointer = substr( str, pos, len);
printf("\nRequired substring is \"%s\"\n", pointer);
free(pointer);
getch();
return 0;
}
char *substr(char *str, int pos, int len)
{
char *pointer;
int i;
pointer = malloc(len+1);
if( pointer == NULL )
{
printf("Unable to allocate memory.\n");
exit(0);
}
for( i = 0 ; i < pos -1 ; i++ )
str++;
for( i = 0 ; i < len ; i++ )
{
*(pointer+i) = *str;
str++;
}
*(pointer+i) = '\0';
return pointer;
}
```

Input:

Enter a string:ACME IT

Enter the position and length of substring:6 2

Output:
Required substring is "IT"

Program -248] Program to find substring of all strings.

```
#include<stdio.h>
#include<conio.h>
#include<string.h>
#include<malloc.h>
char* substr(char*, int, int);
main()
{
char str[100], *pointer;
int pos = 1, len = 1, temp, strlength;
clrscr();
printf("Enter a string:");
gets(str);
temp = strlength = strlen(str);
printf("\nSubstring of \"%s\" are\n", str);
while ( pos <= strlength )
{
while ( len <= temp )
{
pointer = substr(str, pos, len);
printf("%s\n", pointer);
free(pointer);
len++;
}
temp--;
pos++;
len = 1;
}
getch();
return 0;
}
char *substr(char *str, int pos, int len)
{
char *pointer;
```

```
int i;
pointer = malloc(len+1);
if( pointer == NULL )
{
printf("Unable to allocate memory.\n");
exit(0);
}
for( i = 0 ; i < pos -1 ; i++ )
str++;
for( i = 0 ; i < len ; i++ )
{
*(pointer+i) = *str;
str++;
}
*(pointer+i) = '\0';
return pointer;
}
```

Input:

Enter a string:ACME

Output:

Substring of "ACME" are
A
AC
ACM
ACME
C
CM
CME
M
ME
E

Program -249] Sort string alphabetically.

```
#include<stdio.h>
#include<conio.h>
#include<stdlib.h>
#include<string.h>
```

```
main()
{
char str[100], ch, *pointer, *res, *temp;
int c, len;
clrscr();
printf("Enter a string:");
gets(str);
len = strlen(str);
temp = res = (char*)malloc(len+1);
pointer = str;
for ( ch = 'a' ; ch <= 'z' ; ch++ )
{
for ( c = 0 ; c < len ; c++ )
{
if ( *pointer == ch )
{
*res = *pointer;
res++;
}
pointer++;
}
pointer = str;
}
*res = '\0';
res = temp;
strcpy(str, res);
free(res);
printf("%s\n", str);
getch();
return 0;
}
```

Input:

Enter a string:acme

Output:

acem

Program -250] Program to remove blank spaces from string.

```
#include<stdio.h>
#include<conio.h>
#include<string.h>
#include<stdlib.h>
#define SPACE ' '
main()
{
char str[100], *blank, *bgn;
int len, c = 0, d = 0;
clrscr();
printf("Enter a string:");
gets(str);
len = strlen(str);
blank = str;
bgn = (char*)malloc(len+1);
if ( bgn == NULL )
exit(EXIT_FAILURE);
while(*(blank+c))
{
if ( *(blank+c) == SPACE && *(blank+c+1) == SPACE )
{}
else
{
*(bgn+d) = *(blank+c);
d++;
}
c++;
}
*(bgn+d)='\0';
printf("%s",bgn);
free(bgn);
getch();
return 0;
}
```

Input:

Enter a string: ACME IT Consultancy & Services

Output:

ACME IT Consultancy & Services

Program -251] Program to convert string into lowercase using strlwr() function.

```
#include<stdio.h>
#include<conio.h>
#include<string.h>
main()
{
char str[] = "ACME IT CONSULTANCY & SERVICES";
clrscr();
printf("%s\n",strlwr(str));
getch();
return 0;
}
```

Output:

acme it consultancy & services

Program -252] Program to convert string into uppercase using strupr() function.

```
#include<stdio.h>
#include<conio.h>
#include<string.h>
main()
{
char str[] = "acme it consultancy & services";
clrscr();
printf("%s\n",strupr(str));
getch();
return 0;
}
```

Output:

ACME IT CONSULTANCY & SERVICES

Program -253] Program to convert string into uppercase without using strupr()

function.

```
#include<stdio.h>
#include<conio.h>
void ucase(char*);
main()
{
char str[100];
clrscr();
printf("Enter a string to convert it into upper case:");
gets(str);
ucase(str);
printf("Entered string in upper case is \"%s\"\n", str);
getch();
return 0;
}
void ucase(char *str)
{
while(*str)
{
if ( *str >= 97 && *str <= 122 )
{
*str = *str -32;
}
str++;
}
}
```

Input:

Enter a string to convert it into upper case:acme it consultancy & services

Output:

Entered string in upper case is "ACME IT CONSULTANCY & SERVICES"

Program -254] Program to convert string into lowercase without using strlwr()

function.

```
#include<stdio.h>
#include<conio.h>
```

```
void lcase(char*);
main()
{
char str[100];
clrscr();
printf("Enter a string to convert it into lower case:");
gets(str);
lcase(str);
printf("Entered string in lower case is \"%s\"\n", str);
getch();
return 0;
}
void lcase(char *str)
{
while(*str)
{
if ( *str >= 'A' && *str <= 'Z' )
{
*str = *str + 32;
}
str++;
}
}
```

Input:

Enter a string to convert it into lower case:ACME IT

Output:

Entered string in lower case is "acme it"

Program -255] Program to swap two strings.

```
#include<stdio.h>
#include<conio.h>
#include<string.h>
#include<malloc.h>
main()
{
char str1[100], str2[100], *temp;
clrscr();
```

```
printf("\nEnter the first string:");
gets(str1);
printf("\nEnter the second string:");
gets(str2);
printf("\nBefore Swapping\n");
printf("\nFirst string: %s\n",str1);
printf("\nSecond string: %s\n\n",str2);
temp = (char*)malloc(100);
strcpy(temp,str1);
strcpy(str1,str2);
strcpy(str2,temp);
printf("\nAfter Swapping\n");
printf("\nFirst string: %s\n",str1);
printf("\nSecond string: %s\n",str2);
getch();
return 0;
}
```

Input:

Enter the first string:ACME
Enter the second string:IT

Output:

Before Swapping
First string: ACME
Second string: IT
After Swapping
First string: IT
Second string: ACME

Program -256] Program to find occurrence of characters in string.

```
#include<stdio.h>
#include<conio.h>
#include<string.h>
main()
{
char str[100], ch;
int i = 0, cnt[26] = {0};
clrscr();
```

```
printf("\nEnter a string:");
gets(str);
while ( str[i] != '\0' )
{
if ( str[i] >= 'a' && str[i] <= 'z' )
cnt[str[i]-'a']++;
i++;
}
for ( i = 0 ; i < 26 ; i++ )
{
if( cnt[i] != 0 )
printf("%c occurs %d times in the entered string.\n",i+'a',cnt[i]);
}
getch();
return 0;
}
```

Input:

Enter a string:have a nice day

Output:

a occurs 3 times in the entered string.
c occurs 1 times in the entered string.
d occurs 1 times in the entered string.
e occurs 2 times in the entered string.
h occurs 1 times in the entered string.
i occurs 1 times in the entered string.
n occurs 1 times in the entered string.
v occurs 1 times in the entered string.
y occurs 1 times in the entered string.

Program -257] Check whether strings are anagram or not.

Anagram - An anagram of a string is another string that contains same characters, only the order of characters can be different. For example, "pqrs" and "rspq" are anagram of each other.

```
#include<stdio.h>
#include<conio.h>
int anachk(char [], char []);
main()
```

```
{
char str1[100], str2[100];
int flag;
clrscr();
printf("\nEnter first string:");
gets(str1);
printf("\nEnter second string:");
gets(str2);
flag = anachk(str1, str2);
if ( flag == 1 )
printf("\"%s\" and \"%s\" are anagrams.\n", str1, str2);
else
printf("\"%s\" and \"%s\" are not anagrams.\n", str1, str2);
getch();
return 0;
}
int anachk(char s1[], char s2[])
{
int first[26] = {0}, second[26] = {0}, i = 0;
while ( s1[i] != '\0' )
{
first[s1[i]-'a']++;
i++;
}
i = 0;
while (s2[i] != '\0' )
{
second[s2[i]-'a']++;
i++;
}
for ( i = 0 ; i < 26 ; i++ )
{
if( first[i] != second[i] )
return 0;
}
return 1;
}
```

Input:

Enter first string:madam
Enter second string:madam
Output:
"madam" and "madam" are anagrams.

Program -258] Program to replace more than one blank with a single blank.

```
#include<stdio.h>
#include<conio.h>
#include<string.h>
void main()
{
static char s1[]="ACME IT Consultancy And Services";
char s2[50];
char *string,*array;
int j,length;
clrscr();
string=s1 ;
array=s2;
length=strlen(string);
for(j=0;j<=length-1;j++)
{
if(*string==‘ ’)
{
if(*(string+1)!=‘ ’)
{
*array=*string;
array++;
}
string++;
}
else
{
*array=*string;
array++;
string++;
}
```

```
}
*array='\0';
printf("\nOriginal Statement=%s",s1);
printf("\nModified Statement=%s",s2);
getch();
}
```

Output:

Original Statement=ACME IT Consultancy And Services
Modified Statement=ACME IT Consultancy And Services

Program -259] Program to replace a substring.

```
#include<stdio.h>
#include<conio.h>
#include<string.h>
void main()
{
char s1[20];
char s2[20];
char *news,*t,*p;
int j;
char *string[]={"ACME Consultancy And Services"};
clrscr();
printf("Original string is:%s",*string);
printf("\n\nEnter the string to be replace:");
scanf("%s",s1);
printf("\nEnter the new string:");
scanf("%s",s2);
if(strlen(s2)>strlen(s1))
{
printf("\nEnter a string with %d charachters only",strlen(s1));
exit();
}
for(j=0;j<2;i++)
{
p=strstr(string[j],s1);
if(p)
{
```

```
news=p+strlen(s1);
strcpy(t,news);
strcpy(p,s2);
strcat(p,t);
break;
}
}
printf("\nThe new string is:");
for(j=0;j<1;j++)
printf("\n%s",string[j]);
getch();
}
```

Input:

Original string is:ACME Consultancy And Services
Enter the string to be replace:And
Enter the new string:&

Output:

The new string is:
ACME Consultancy & Services

Program -260] Program to reverse string stored in an array of pointers.

```
#include<stdio.h>
#include<conio.h>
#include<string.h>
void revstr(char*);
void main()
{
static char *string[]={"ACME IT Consultancy And Services"};
int j;
clrscr();
for(j=0;j<1;j++)
{
revstr(string[j]);
printf("\n%s",string[j]);
}
getch();
}
```

```
void revstr(char *str)
{
int k,l;
char *tar,temp;
l=strlen(str);
tar=str+l-1;
for(k=0;k<=l/2;k++)
{
temp=*str;
*str=*tar;
*tar=temp;
str++;
tar--;
}
}
```

Output:

secivreS dnA ycantlusnoC TI EMCA

Program -261] Program to delete all vowels from a sentence.

```
#include<stdio.h>
#include<conio.h>
#include<string.h>
void main()
{
char s1[80],s2[80];
char *o,*n;
clrscr();
printf("\nEnter a sentence not more than 80 characters long:");
gets(s1);
o=s1;
n=s2;
while(*o)
{
if(*o=='a'||*o=='e'||*o=='i'||*o=='o'||*o=='u')
o++;
else
if(*o=='A'||*o=='E'||*o=='I'||*o=='O'||*o=='U')
```

```
o++;
else
*n++=*o++;
}
*n='\0';
printf("\n\nSentence after removing all vowels is:");
puts(s2);
getch();
}
```

Input:

Enter a sentence not more than 80 characters long:ACME IT

Output:

Sentence after removing all vowels is:CM T

Program -262] Program to delete all occurrences of "an" from a sentence.

```
#include<stdio.h>
#include<conio.h>
#include<string.h>
void main()
{
char first[80],array[80];
char *x,*q,*p;
int i;
clrscr();
printf("\nEnter a sentence upto 80 characters :");
gets(first);
x=first;
p=array;
while(*x)
{
q=x;
if(*x=='a'||*x=='A')
{
x++;
if(*x=='n'||*x=='N')
{
x++;
```

```
}
else
{
*p++=*q++;
x--;
}
}
else
*p++=*x;
x++;
}
*p='\0';
printf("\n\n Resultant Sentence is :");
puts(array);
getch();
}
```

Input:

Enter a sentence upto 80 characters : an the key to success

Output:

Resultant Sentence is : the key to success

Program -263] Progam to count the no of lowercase and uppercase alphabet in an entered text.

```
#include<stdio.h>
#include<conio.h>
#include<string.h>
main()
{
char string[20];
int j,ucase=0,lcase=0;
clrscr();
printf("Enter text or sentences:");
gets(string);
for(j=0;string[j]!='\0';j++)
{
if(isupper(string[j]))
```

```
{
ucase=ucase+1;
}
else
{
lcase=lcase+1;
}
continue;
}
printf("Number of upper case:%d \n Number of lower
case:%d",ucase,lcase);
getch();
return(0);
}
```

Input:

Enter your text:ACME IT Consultancy And Services

Output:

Number of upper case:9

Number of lower case:23

Program -264] Program to read a string and capatalise the first character of every word.

```
#include<stdio.h>
#include<conio.h>
#include<string.h>
void main()
{
char string[80];
int j;
clrscr();
printf("\nEnter the string:");
scanf("%s",&string);
string[0]=toupper(string[0]);
j=1;
while(string[j]!='\0')
{
```

```
if(string[j]==' ')
string[j+1]=toupper(string[j+1]);
j++;
}
printf("\nThe modified string is:");
puts(string);
getch();
}
```

Input:

Enter the string:acme

Output:

The modified string is:Acme

Program -265] Program to determine how many characters, digits, white spaces and other kind of character from given word.

```
#include<stdio.h>
#include<conio.h>
#include<string.h>
void main()
{
char string[80],a;
int i,letter=0,digit=0,space=0,special=0,no;
clrscr();
printf("\nEnter the string:");
gets(string);
no=strlen(string);
for(i=0;i<no;i++)
{
a=string[i];
if(a==' ')
space++;
else if((a>='0') && (a<='9'))
digit++;
else if(((a>='A') && (a<='Z')) || ((a>='a') && (a<='z')))
letter++;
else
```

```
special++;
}
printf("\nDigits:%d",digit);
printf("\nLetters:%d",letter);
printf("\nSpaces:%d",space);
printf("\nSpecial Character:%d",special);
getch();
}
```

Input:

Enter the string:ACME IT Consultancy & Services

Output:

Digits:0

Letters:25

Spaces:4

Special Character:1

Program -266] Program of using function read & write string.

```
#include<stdio.h>
#include<conio.h>
void main()
{
char sent[100];
clrscr();
iputs("Enter a sentence:");
igets(sent);
printf("\n");
iputs(sent);
getch();
}
iputs(char *s1)
{
while(*s1)
{
putch(*s1);
s1++;
}
return 1;
```

```
}
igets(char *s1)
{
int i;
char ch;
for(i=0;i<=98;i++)
{
ch=getche();
if(ch=='\r')
{
*s1='\0';
break;
}
if(ch=='\b')
{
printf("\b");
i--;
s1--;
}
else
{
*s1=ch;
s1++;
}
}
return 1;
}
```

CHAPTER SIXTEEN

Structure Programs

Program -267] Program to add two complex numbers.

```
#include<stdio.h>
#include<conio.h>
#include<stdlib.h>
struct complex
{
int real;
int img;
};
main()
{
struct complex x,y,z;
clrscr();
printf("Enter a and b where a + ib:");
printf("\na = ");
scanf("%d", &x.real);
printf("b = ");
scanf("%d", &x.img);
printf("Enter c and d where c + id: ");
printf("\nc = ");
scanf("%d", &y.real);
printf("d = ");
scanf("%d", &y.img);
z.real = x.real + y.real;
z.img = x.img + y.img;
if ( z.img >= 0 )
printf("Sum of two complex nos = %d + %di",z.real,z.img);
getch();
```

```
return 0;
}
```

Program -268] Program to create structure to store student data.

```
#include<stdio.h>
#include<conio.h>
#include<string.h>
struct studinfo
{
int rollno;
char sname[20];
char dept[20];
char course[20];
int year;
};
struct studinfo s[2];
void enter_student_data();
void displayinfo();
void find_stud(int);
void main()
{
int i,r,y;
clrscr();
printf("\nEnter the data of each student:");
enter_student_data();
displayinfo();
printf("\nEnter the year of joining of the student");
scanf("%d",&y);
find_stud(y);
getch();
}
void enter_student_data()
{
int i;
for(i=0;i<2;i++)
{
printf("\nEnter Student Data:");
```

```
printf("\n-------------------------");
printf("\nRoll number:");
scanf("%d",&s[i].rollno);
printf("\nName:");
scanf("%s",&s[i].sname);
printf("\nDepartment:");
scanf("%s",&s[i].dept);
printf("\nCourse:");
scanf("%s",&s[i].course);
printf("\nYear:");
scanf("%d",&s[i].year);
}
}
void displayinfo()
{
int i;
for(i=0;i<2;i++)
{
printf("\nStudent Data:");
printf("\n-------------------------");
printf("\nRoll number:%d",s[i].rollno);
printf("\nName:%s",s[i].sname);
printf("\nDepartment:%s",s[i].dept);
printf("\nCourse:%s",s[i].course);
printf("\nYear:%d",s[i].year);
}
}
void find_stud(int y)
{
int i,j=0;
for(i=0;i<2;i++)
{
if(y==s[i].year)
{
printf("%s joined in the year %d\n",s[i].sname,s[i].year);
j=1;
}
if(j==0)
```

```
printf("\n No student joined %d",y);
}
}
```

Program -269] Program to create structure for store customers bank account detail.

```
#include<stdio.h>
#include<conio.h>
struct customer
{
int acno;
char name[20];
float bal;
};
struct customer cust[1];
void withdrawal_amt(int acno,float amount);
void department(int acno,float amount);
void depamt(int acno,float amount);
void displayinfo();
void cust_data();
void main()
{
int i,ano,choice;
float amount;
clrscr();
cust_data();
displayinfo();
printf("\n\nEnter the account number and the amount to be
deposited/withdrawn:");
printf("\nAccount number:");
scanf("%d",&ano);
printf("\nAmount:");
scanf("%f",&amount);
department(ano,amount);
displayinfo();
getch();
```

```
}
void department(int acno,float amount)
{
int ch;
printf("\n\nEnter 1 for Deposite\tEnter 2 for withdrawal:");
scanf("%d",&ch);
switch(ch)
{
case 1:
depamt(acno,amount);
break;
case 2:
withdrawal_amt(acno,amount);
break;
default:
printf("\n\nYou entered wrong choice");
}
}
void depamt(int acno,float amount)
{
int i,j=0;
for(i=0;i<1;i++)
{
if(cust[i].acno==acno)
{
cust[i].bal+=amount;
j=1;
}
}
if(j==0)
printf("\n\nWrong Account Number");
}
void withdrawal_amt(int acno,float amount)
{
int i,j=0;
for(i=0;i<1;i++)
{
if(cust[i].acno==acno)
```

```
{
j=1;
if(cust[i].bal<100)
{
printf("\n\nThe balance is insufficient for withdrawal");
getch();
}
else
if(cust[i].bal-100>=amount)
cust[i].bal-=amount;
else
printf("\n\nWithdrawal amount less than or equal to %f Rs",cust[i].bal-
100);
}
}
if(j==0)
printf("\n Wrong Account Number ");
}
void displayinfo()
{
int i;
for(i=0;i<1;i++)
{
printf("\n\nCustomer Data:");
printf("\n-------------------------");
printf("\nCustomer number:%d",i+1);
printf("\nAccount number:%d",cust[i].acno);
printf("\nName:%s",cust[i].name);
printf("\nBalance Amount:%f",cust[i].bal);
}
}
void cust_data()
{
int i;
for(i=0;i<1;i++)
{
printf("\nEnter Customer Data:");
printf("\n-------------------------");
```

```
printf("\nAccount Number:");
scanf("%d",&cust[i].acno);
printf("\nName:");
scanf("%s",&cust[i].name);
printf("\nBalance Amount:");
scanf("%f",&cust[i].bal);
clrscr();
}
}
```

Program -270] Program to create structure to store engine parts data.

```
#include<stdio.h>
#include<conio.h>
struct automobile
{
int sno;
int year;
char mate[20];
int qty;
};
struct automobile p[1];
void auto_data();
void findrec();
void displayinfo();
void main()
{
int i;
clrscr();
auto_data();
displayinfo();
findrec();
getch();
}
void findrec()
{
int i,j;
printf("\n\nEnter List of parts between A1 & A6:");
```

```
for(i=0;i<1;i++)
{
if((p[i].sno>0xa1)&&(p[i].sno<=0xa6))
{
j=1;
printf("\n\nPart Number:%d",i);
printf("\n\nSerial Number:%x",p[i].sno);
printf("\n\nYear of manufacturing:%d",p[i].year);
printf("\n\nMaterial Used:%s",p[i].mate);
printf("\n\nManufacture Quantity:%d",p[i].qty);
}
}
if(j==0)
{
printf("\n\nNo Such Record Present");
}
}
void displayinfo()
{
int i;
for(i=0;i<1;i++)
{
printf("\n\nEngine Parts Data:");
printf("\n-------------------------");
printf("\nPart number:%d",i);
printf("\nSerial number:%x",p[i].sno);
printf("\nYear of manufacturing:%d",p[i].year);
printf("\nMaterial Used:%s",p[i].mate);
printf("\nManufacture Quantity:%d",p[i].qty);
}
}
void auto_data()
{
int i;
for(i=0;i<1;i++)
{
while(1)
{
```

```
printf("\nEnter the serial number of the part");
printf("\nNumber must be between A1 and A9:");
scanf("%x",&p[i].sno);
if(p[i].sno>=0xA1 && p[i].sno<=0xA6)
break;
}
printf("\nEnter the Year of Manufacturing of the part:");
scanf("%d",&p[i].year);
printf("\nEnter the material of the part:");
scanf("%s",&p[i].mate);
printf("\nEnter the quantity of the part:");
scanf("%d",&p[i].qty);
clrscr();
}
}
```

Program -271] Program to create structure and compare the dates.

```
#include<stdio.h>
#include<conio.h>
struct date
{
int d,m,y;
};
int chkdate(struct date *dt);
void main()
{
int chkdt;
struct date d1,d2;
clrscr();
printf("\nEnter the dates to be compared:");
chkdt=chkdate(&d1);
if(chkdt==0)
exit();
chkdt=chkdate(&d2);
if(chkdt==0)
exit();
if((d1.d==d2.d)&&(d1.m==d2.m)&&(d1.y==d2.y))
```

```
printf("\nGiven dates are equal");
else
printf("\nGiven dates are different");
getch();
}
int chkdate(struct date *dt)
{
printf("\nEnter date(dd):");
scanf("%d",&dt->d);
printf("\nEnter month(mm):");
scanf("%d",&dt->m);
printf("\nEnter the year(yyyy");
scanf("%d",&dt->y);
if((dt->d>31||dt->d<0)||(dt->m>12||dt->m<0)||(dt-
>y>9999||dt->y<1000))
{
printf("Invalid date format...");
return (0);
}
else
return (1);
}
```

Program -272] Program to calculate net salary using structure.

```
#include<stdio.h>
#include<conio.h>
struct employee
{
char ename[20];
char ecode[6];
float basic;
float hra,da;
float netpay;
}emp[50];
void main()
{
float j,n;
```

```
clrscr();
printf("How many record do you want:");
scanf("%f",&n);
for(j=0;j<n;j++)
{
printf("\nEnter name of employee:");
scanf("%s",&emp[j].ename);
printf("\nEnter ecode:");
scanf("%s",&emp[j].ecode);
printf("\nEnter basic pay:");
scanf("%f",&emp[j].basic);
printf("\nEnter HRA:");
scanf("%f",&emp[j].hra);
printf("\nEnter DA:");
scanf("%f",&emp[j].da);
}
for(j=0;j<n;j++)
{
emp[j].netpay=emp[j].basic+emp[j].hra+emp[j].da;
printf("\nName:%s",emp[j].ename);
printf("\nEcode:%s",emp[j].ecode);
printf("\nBasic Pay:%.2f",emp[j].basic);
printf("\nHRA:%.2f",emp[j].hra);
printf("\nDA:%.2f",emp[j].da);
printf("\nNet Pay:%.2f",emp[j].netpay);
}
getch();
}
```

CHAPTER SEVENTEEN

Console Program

Program -273] Program of using a function getint().

```
#include<stdio.h>
#include<conio.h>
void main()
{
int x;
clrscr();
printf("Enter a numeric string:");
x=getint();
printf("\n\nYou Entered:%d",x);
getch();
}
getint()
{
char string[6];
int i,j,k,val;
i=0;
while(i<=5)
{
string[i]=getche();
if(string[i]=='\r')
{
string[i]='\0';
break;
}
if(string[i]=='\b')
{
i--;
```

```
printf("\b");
}
else
i++;
}
val=0;
k=1;
for(j=i-1;j>=0;j--)
{
val=val+(string[j]-48)*k;
k=k*10;
}
return(val);
}
xgets(char *s)
{
int i;
char ch;
for(i=0;i<=98;i++)
{
ch=getche();
if(ch=='\r')
{
*s='\0';
break;
}
if(ch=='\b')
{
printf("\b");
i--;
s--;
}
else
{
*s=ch;
s++;
}
}
```

```
return (*s);
}
```

CHAPTER EIGHTEEN

File Handling Programs

Program -274] Program Read a file.

```
#include<stdio.h>
#include<conio.h>
#include<stdlib.h>
main()
{
char ch, filename[25];
FILE *filepointer;
clrscr();
printf("Enter the name of file you wish to see:");
gets(filename);
filepointer = fopen(filename,"r");
if( filepointer == NULL )
{
perror("Error ");
printf("Press any key to exit...");
getch();
exit(1);
}
printf("The contents of %s file are :- \n\n",filename);
while( ( ch = fgetc(filepointer) ) != EOF)
printf("%c",ch);
getch();
fclose(filepointer);
return 0;
}
```

Program -275] Program to perform copy file operation.

```
#include<stdio.h>
#include<conio.h>
#include<stdlib.h>
int main()
{
char ch, f1[20], f2[20];
FILE *fs,*ft;
clrscr();
printf("Enter name of file to copy:");
gets(f1);
fs = fopen(f1,"r");
if( fs == NULL )
{
perror("Error ");
printf("Press any key to exit...\n");
getch();
exit(EXIT_FAILURE);
}
printf("Enter name of target file: ");
gets(f2);
ft = fopen(f2,"w");
if( ft == NULL )
{
perror("Error ");
fclose(fs);
printf("Press any key to exit...\n");
getch();
exit(EXIT_FAILURE);
}
while( ( ch = fgetc(fs) ) != EOF )
fputc(ch,ft);
printf("File copied successfully.\n");
getch();
fclose(fs);
fclose(ft);
return 0;
}
```

Program -276] Program to perform two files merge operation.

```
#include<stdio.h>
#include<conio.h>
#include<stdlib.h>
main()
{
FILE *files1, *files2, *ft;
char ch, f1[20], f2[20], f3[20];
clrscr();
printf("Enter name of first file:");
gets(f1);
printf("\nEnter name of second file:");
gets(f2);
printf("\nEnter name of file which will store contents of two files:");
gets(f3);
files1 = fopen(f1,"r");
files2 = fopen(f2,"r");
if( files1 == NULL || files2 == NULL )
{
perror("Error ");
printf("Press any key to exit...\n");
getch();
exit(EXIT_FAILURE);
}
ft = fopen(f3,"w");
if( ft == NULL )
{
perror("Error ");
printf("Press any key to exit...\n");
exit(EXIT_FAILURE);
}
while( ( ch = fgetc(files1) ) != EOF )
fputc(ch,ft);
while( ( ch = fgetc(files2) ) != EOF )
fputc(ch,ft);
printf("\nTwo files were merged into %s file successfully.\n",f3);
```

```
fclose(files1);
fclose(files2);
fclose(ft);
getch();
return 0;
}
```

Program -277] Program to display files in the current directory.

```
#include<stdio.h>
#include<conio.h>
#include<dir.h>
main()
{
int done;
struct ffblk a;
clrscr();
printf("\nPress any key to continue");
getch();
done = findfirst("*.*",&a,0);
while(!done)
{
printf("%s\n",a.ff_name);
done = findnext(&a);
}
getch();
return 0;
}
```

Program -278] Program to perform file delete operation.

```
#include<stdio.h>
#include<conio.h>
int main()
{
int chkst;
char filename[25];
clrscr();
```

```
printf("Enter the name of file to delete:");
gets(filename);
chkst = remove(filename);
if( chkst == 0 )
printf("%s file deleted successfully\n",filename);
else
{
printf("Unable to delete the file\n");
perror("Error ");
}
getch();
return 0;
}
```

Program -279] Program to display a file with line number.

```
#include<stdio.h>
#include<conio.h>
void main()
{
FILE *filepointer;
char ch;
char filename[67];
int cnt=1;
clrscr();
printf("Enter a file name:");
gets(filename);
filepointer=fopen(filename,"r");
if(filepointer==NULL)
{
puts("Unable to open the file");
getch();
exit();
}
printf("\n\nFile Name:%s",filename);
printf("\nLine:%d",cnt);
while((ch=getc(filepointer))!=EOF)
{
```

```
if(ch=='\n')
{
cnt++;
printf("\nLine No : %d",cnt);
}
else
printf("%c",ch);
}
getch();
fclose(filepointer);
}
```

Program -280] Program to find the size of a text file.

```
#include<stdio.h>
#include<conio.h>
struct filesize
{
char filename[20];
char txt[3];
char username[20];
long int size;
};
struct filesize f[16];
void main()
{
int i,j,c;
char fname[20];
char ch=1,len,len1;
clrscr();
absread(0,1,5,f);
for(i=0;i<16;i++)
printf("%s %s %ld\n",f[i].filename,f[i].txt,f[i].size);
printf("Enter the file name:");
scanf("%s",&fname);
len1=len=strlen(name);
i=0;
while(i<16)
```

```
{
while(len--!=0)
{
if(f[i].filename[len]==fname[len])
ch=0;
else
{
ch=1;
break;
}
}
if(ch==0 && len==-1)
break;
len=len1;
i++;
}
if(ch==0)
{
printf("%s",f[i].filename);
printf("\t%ld bytes",f[i].size);
}
else
printf("h");
}
```

Program -281] Program to display the content of a file.

```
#include<stdio.h>
#include<conio.h>
void box(int,int,int,int);
void main()
{
FILE *filepointer;
char ch,filename[20];
int pg=1,r=2,c=1;
clrscr();
printf("\nEnter the file name:");
gets(filename);
```

```
clrscr();
filepointer=fopen(filename,"r");
if(fp==NULL)
{
puts("Unable to open source");
getch();
exit(0);
}
printf("gft");
box(1,0,22,79);
gotoxy(0,0);
printf("Filename:%s",filename);
gotoxy(65,0);
printf("Page:%d",pg);
while((ch=getc(fp))!=EOF)
{
if(ch!='\n')
{
gotoxy(r,c);
printf("%c",ch);
c++;
}
else
{
r++;
c=1;
if(r>20)
{
pg++;
r=2;
gotoxy(0,23);
getch();
box(1,0,22,79);
gotoxy(0,0);
printf("Filename:%s",filename);
gotoxy(65,0);
printf("Page:%d",pg);
}
```

```
}
}
getch();
fclose(fp);
}
void box(int a,int b,int i,int j)
{
int x,k;
gotoxy(b,a);
printf("%c",201);
gotoxy(b,i);
printf("%c",202);
gotoxy(j,i);
printf("%c",188);
gotoxy(j,a);
printf("%c",187);
for(x=a+1;x<=i-1;x++)
{
gotoxy(b,x);
printf("%c",186);
gotoxy(j,x);
printf("%c",186);
}
for(k=b+1;k<=j-1;k++)
{
gotoxy(k,a);
printf("%c",205);
gotoxy(k,i);
printf("%c",205);
}
}
```

Program -282] Program to read a file in binary mode and display its content.

```
#include<stdio.h>
#include<conio.h>
struct student
```

```
{
char sname[20];
char address[20];
int age;
char bloodtype;
};
struct student school;
void main()
{
FILE *fp;
char f1[20],f2[20];
int i;
clrscr();
printf("\nEnter the file name:");
gets(f1);
fp=fopen(f1,"wb");
if(fp==NULL)
{
puts("Unable to open source");
getch();
exit(0);
}
for(i=0;i<2;i++)
{
printf("\nName:");
scanf("%s",&school.sname);
fflush(stdin);
printf("\nadd:");
scanf("%s",&school.address);
fflush(stdin);
printf("\nage:");
scanf("%d",&school.age);
fflush(stdin);
printf("\ntype:");
scanf("%c",&school.bloodtype);
fflush(stdin);
fwrite(&school,sizeof(school),1,fp);
}
```

```
fclose(fp);
getch();
printf("\nEnter the file name:");
gets(f2);
fp=fopen(f2,"rb");
if(fp==NULL)
{
puts("Unable to open source");
getch();
exit(0);
}
while(fread(&school,sizeof(school),1,fp)==1)
{
if(school.age<25 && school.bloodtype=='2')
printf("\n%s %s %d
%c",school.sname,school.address,school.age,school.bloodtype);
}
fclose(fp);
getch();
}
```

Program -283] Program to create a file on disk, retrive data as required.

```
#include<stdio.h>
#include<conio.h>
void main()
{
FILE *fp;
char filename[20],empname[20],ch,choice='y';
int num,n;
clrscr();
printf("\nEnter the file name:");
gets(filename);
fp=fopen(filename,"w+");
if(fp==NULL)
{
puts("Unable to open source");
getch();
```

```
exit(0);
}
while(choice=='y'|| choice=='Y')
{
printf("\nEnter the employee name:");
scanf("%s",&empname);
fputs(empname,fp);
fputs("\n",fp);
puts("Do you want to add more name y/n:");
fflush(stdin);
choice=getch();
}
fseek(fp,0L,SEEK_SET);
puts("\nEnter any number from the list:");
scanf("%d",&num);
n=num;
while(fgets(empname,21,fp)!=NULL)
{
num--;
if(num==0)
printf("The name of employee no.%d is:%s",n,empname);
}
if(num>0)
puts("No such number exits in the list");
fseek(fp,0L,SEEK_SET);
puts("\nThe list of employee whose name start with S are:");
while(fgets(empname,21,fp)!=NULL)
{
if(empname[0]=='s'||empname[0]=='S')
printf("%s",empname);
}
fclose(fp);
getch();
}
```

Program -284] Program to count total number of words in a file.

```
#include<stdio.h>
```

```
#include<conio.h>
#include<string.h>
void main()
{
FILE *fp;
char filename[20],s[80];
int wordcnt=0,flwcnt=0,i;
clrscr();
printf("\nEnter the file name:");
gets(filename);
fp=fopen(filename,"r");
if(fp==NULL)
{
puts("Unable to open file");
getch();
exit(0);
}
while(fgets(str,79,fp)!=NULL)
{
for(i=1;s[i]!='\0';i++)
{
if(s[i]=='.' || (s[i]=='\n' && s[i-1]!='.')||
s[i]==','||(s[i]==' ' && s[i-1]!=',' &&
s[i-1]!='.'))
wordcnt++;
if(i<74)
{
if(s[i]==' ' && (s[i+5]==' '
||s[i+5]=='\n'||s[i+5]=='.'||
s[i+5]==','))
flwcnt++;
if(i==1&&(s[4]==' '||s[4]==','||s[4]=='.')
&&(s[1]!=' ' &&s[1]!=','&&s[1]!='.')
&&(s[2]!=' ' && s[2]!=' ' &&s[2]!=',' && s[2]!='.'))
flwcnt++;
}
}
}
```

```
clrscr();
printf("\nThe total number of words are %d",wordcnt);
printf("\nThe number of four letter words are %d",flwcnt);
fclose(fp);
getch();
}
```

Program -285] Program to read a text file and print each word in reverse order.

```
#include<stdio.h>
#include<conio.h>
#include<string.h>
void main()
{
FILE *fp;
char filename[20],s[80],ch;
int i=0;
clrscr();
printf("\nEnter the file name:");
gets(filename);
fp=fopen(filename,"r");
if(fp==NULL)
{
puts("Unable to open file");
getch();
exit(0);
}
while((ch=getc(fp))!=EOF)
{
if(ch=='\n'||ch==' ')
{
s[i]='\0';
strrev(s);
printf("%s ",s);
i=0;
}
else
```

```
s[i++]=ch;
}
fclose(fp);
getch();
}
}
```

CHAPTER NINETEEN

Command Line Argument Programs

Program -286] Program to search for a word in a file and replace it with the specified word.

```
#include<stdio.h>
#include<conio.h>
#include<string.h>
FILE *fs,*ft;
void main(int argc,char *argv[])
{
char str[80];
char *arg1,*arg2,*filename;
int newstr(char *s,char *t,char *n);
int c=0;
clrscr();
if(argc!=4)
{
puts("improper number of arguments");
exit();
}
fs=fopen(argv[3],"r+");
ft=fopen("s2.txt","w");
if(fs==NULL)
{
puts("Unable to open file");
getch();
exit(0);
```

```
}
if(strlen(argv[1])>strlen(argv[2]))
{
printf("\nNumber of charcters in string mismatch");
}
arg1=argv[1];
arg2=argv[2];
filename=argv[3];
while(fgets(str,79,fs)!=NULL)
c=newstr(str,arg1,arg2);
fclose(fs);
fclose(ft);
printf("\n%d Replacements of words done successfully.",c);
remove(filename);
rename("s2.txt",filename);
getch();
}
int newstr(char *pt,char *t,char *n)
{
static int count=0;
char *p,*temp,*news,*p1;
p1=pt;
do
{
p=strstr(p1,t);
if(p==NULL)
break;
news=p+strlen(t);
strcpy(temp,news);
strcpy(p,n);
strcat(p,temp);
count++;
p1=p1+strlen(t);
}
while(1);
fputs(pt,ft);
return count;
}
```

Program -287] Program to perform the given arithmetic operation on the two integers.

```
#include<stdio.h>
#include<conio.h>
#include<string.h>
void main(int argc,char *argv[])
{
int i,no1,no2,ans;
char *str[7]={"+","-","*","/","%","&&","||"};
clrscr();
if(argc!=4)
{
puts("improper number of arguments");
exit();
}
for(i=0;i<=6;i++)
{
if(strcmp(argv[2],str[i])==0)
break;
}
if(i==7)
{
printf("\nNot a valid operator");
exit();
}
first=atoi(argv[1]);
second=atoi(argv[3]);
printf("\nResult of the operation is:");
switch(i)
{
case 0:
ans=no1+no2;
printf("\nAddition is :%d",ans);
break;
case 1:
```

```
ans=no1-no2;
printf("\ Substraction is :%d",ans);
break;
case 2:
ans=no1*no2;
printf("\n Multiplication is :%d",ans);
break;
case 3:
ans=no1/no2;
printf("\nDivision is:%d",ans);
break;
case 4:
ans=no1%no2;
printf("\nMod is:%d",ans);
break;
case 5:
ans=no1&&no2;
ans==0?printf("\nFalse"):printf("\nTrue");
break;
case 6:
ans=no1||no2;
ans==0?printf("\nFalse"):printf("\nTrue");
break;
}
getch();
}
```

CHAPTER TWENTY

Graphics Program

Note - Please check graphics path as per your Turboc3 / C Installer. e.g "C:\\TC\\BGI"

Program -288] Program perform draw different shapes.

```
#include<graphics.h>
#include<conio.h>
main()
{
int gd = DETECT,gm;
initgraph(&gd, &gm, "C:\\TC\\BGI");
rectangle(100,100,150,150);
circle(150,300,45);
bar(250,200,180,140);
line(350,250,650,250);
ellipse(350,100,120,100,50,70);
outtextxy(200,430,"Draw Different Shapes");
getch();
closegraph();
return 0;
}
```

Program -289] Bar Chart.

```
#include<graphics.h>
#include<conio.h>
main()
{
int gd = DETECT, gm;
initgraph(&gd, &gm, "C:\\TC\\BGI");
```

```
setcolor(RED);
rectangle(40,40,600,420);
settextstyle(SANS_SERIF_FONT,HORIZ_DIR,2);
setcolor(WHITE);
outtextxy(100,0,"Bar Chart");
setlinestyle(SOLID_LINE,0,2);
line(100,420,100,60);
line(100,420,600,420);
line(90,70,100,60);
line(110,70,100,60);
line(590,410,600,420);
line(590,430,600,420);
outtextxy(95,35,"Y");
outtextxy(610,405,"X");
outtextxy(85,415,"O");
setfillstyle(LINE_FILL,RED);
bar(150,100,200,419);
setfillstyle(XHATCH_FILL,GREEN);
bar(225,150,275,419);
setfillstyle(WIDE_DOT_FILL,BLUE);
bar(300,200,350,419);
setfillstyle(INTERLEAVE_FILL,BROWN);
bar(375,125,425,419);
setfillstyle(HATCH_FILL,RED);
bar(450,175,500,419);
setfillstyle(HATCH_FILL,BLUE);
bar(520,50,570,419);
getch();
return 0;
}
```

Program -290] Circles in Circle.

```
#include<graphics.h>
#include<conio.h>
#include<dos.h>
main()
{
```

```
int gd = DETECT, gm, x, y, color, angle = 0;
struct arccoordstype a, b;
initgraph(&gd, &gm, "C:\\TC\\BGI");
delay(2000);
while(angle<=360)
{
setcolor(BLACK);
arc(getmaxx()/2,getmaxy()/2,angle,angle+2,50);
setcolor(BLUE);
getarccoords(&a);
circle(a.xstart,a.ystart,25);
setcolor(BLACK);
arc(getmaxx()/2,getmaxy()/2,angle,angle+2,100);
setcolor(RED);
getarccoords(&a);
circle(a.xstart,a.ystart,25);
setcolor(BLACK);
arc(getmaxx()/2,getmaxy()/2,angle,angle+2,150);
getarccoords(&a);
setcolor(GREEN);
circle(a.xstart,a.ystart,25);
setcolor(BLACK);
arc(getmaxx()/2,getmaxy()/2,angle,angle+2,200);
getarccoords(&a);
setcolor(MAGENTA);
circle(a.xstart,a.ystart,25);
setcolor(BLACK);
arc(getmaxx(),getmaxy(),angle,angle+2,100);
getarccoords(&a);
setcolor(GREEN);
circle(a.xstart,a.ystart,25);
setcolor(BLACK);
arc(getmaxx()-650,getmaxy(),angle,angle+2,100);
getarccoords(&a);
setcolor(GREEN);
circle(a.xstart,a.ystart,25);
setcolor(BLACK);
arc(getmaxx(),getmaxy()-500,angle,angle+2,120);
```

```
getarccoords(&a);
setcolor(GREEN);
circle(a.xstart,a.ystart,25);
setcolor(BLACK);
arc(getmaxx()-680,getmaxy()-460,angle,angle+2,120);
getarccoords(&a);
setcolor(GREEN);
circle(a.xstart,a.ystart,25);
angle = angle+5;
delay(50);
}
getch();
closegraph();
return 0;
}
```

Program -291] Program for draw ellipse.

```
#include<graphics.h>
#include<conio.h>
main()
{
int gd = DETECT, gm,l,t,h,w;
initgraph(&gd, &gm, "C:\\TC\\BGI");
printf("Enter Left side distance -");
scanf("%d",&l);
printf("Enter Distance from side -");
scanf("%d",&t);
printf("Enter Hieght of ellipse -");
scanf("%d",&h);
printf("Enter Width of ellipse -");
scanf("%d",&w);
ellipse(l,t, 0, 360, h,w);
getch();
closegraph();
return 0;
}
```

Program -292] Program for line.

```
#include<graphics.h>
#include<conio.h>
main()
{
int gd = DETECT, gm,l,t,x,y;
initgraph(&gd, &gm, "C:\\TC\\BGI");
printf("Enter left distance \n");
scanf("%d",&l);
printf("Enter top distance \n");
scanf("%d",&t);
printf("Enter X-axis position \n");
scanf("%d",&x);
printf("Enter Y-axis position \n");
scanf("%d",&y);
line(l,t,x,y);
getch();
closegraph();
return 0;
}
```

Program -293] Program for get Color.

```
#include<graphics.h>
#include<conio.h>
main()
{
int gd = DETECT,dc,gm;
char b[100];
initgraph(&gd,&gm,"C:\\TC\\BGI");
dc = getcolor();
sprintf(b,"Current drawing color = %d", dc);
outtextxy(50,50, b );
getch();
closegraph();
return 0;
}
```

Program -294] Program to draw a circle.

```
#include<graphics.h>
#include<conio.h>
main()
{
int gd = DETECT, gm,l,t,r;
initgraph(&gd, &gm, "C:\\TC\\BGI");
printf("Enter Left side distance -");
scanf("%d",&l);
printf("Enter Distance from side -");
scanf("%d",&t);
printf("Enter Radius of circle -");
scanf("%d",&r);
circle(l,t,r);
getch();
closegraph();
return 0;
}
```

Program -295] Program of arc.

```
#include<graphics.h>
#include<conio.h>
main()
{
int gd = DETECT, gm;
initgraph(&gd, &gm, "C:\\TC\\BGI");
arc(100, 100, 0, 135, 50);
getch();
closegraph();
return 0;
}
```

Program -296] Program to draw a bar.

```
#include<graphics.h>
```

```
#include<conio.h>
main()
{
int gd = DETECT, gm;
int l,t,h,w;
initgraph(&gd, &gm, "C:\\TC\\BGI");
printf("Enter Left side distance :\n");
scanf("%d",&l);
printf("Enter Top side distance :\n");
scanf("%d",&t);
printf("Enter Height of bar :\n");
scanf("%d",&h);
printf("Enter Width of bar :\n");
scanf("%d",&w);
bar(l,t,w,h);
getch();
closegraph();
return 0;
}
```

Program -297] Program for draw polygon.

```
#include<graphics.h>
#include<conio.h>
int main()
{
int gd=DETECT, gm, points[]={320,150,520,300,350,300,320,150};
initgraph(&gd,&gm,"C:\\TC\\BGI");
drawpoly(4, points);
getch();
closegraph();
return(0);
}
```

Program -298] Program for fill polygone shape.

```
#include<graphics.h>
#include<conio.h>
```

```
main()
{
int gd=DETECT, gm, points[]={320,150,520,300,350,300,320,150};
initgraph(&gd, &gm, "C:\\TC\\BGI");
fillpoly(4, points);
getch();
closegraph();
return 0;
}
```

CHAPTER TWENTY-ONE

Windows Programs

Program -299] Program for gettime.

```
#include<stdio.h>
#include<conio.h>
#include<dos.h>
main()
{
struct time t1;
clrscr();
gettime(&t1);
printf("System time is %d : %d : %d\n",t1.ti_hour,t1.ti_min,t1.ti_sec);
getch();
return 0;
}
```

Program -300] To Display Mouse Pointer In Textmode.

```
#include<dos.h>
#include<conio.h>
int initmouse();
void showmptr();
union REGS i, o;
main()
{
int conect;
conect = mouseavai();
if ( conect == 0 )
printf("Please check mouse connection...\n");
else
```

```
showmptr();
getch();
return 0;
}
int mouseavai()
{
i.x.ax = 0;
int86(0X33,&i,&o);
return ( o.x.ax );
}
void showmptr()
{
i.x.ax = 1;
int86(0X33,&i,&o);
}
```

Program -301] Program for getdate.

```
#include<stdio.h>
#include<conio.h>
#include<dos.h>
main()
{
struct date da;
clrscr();
getdate(&da);
printf("System date is %d/%d/%d\n",da.da_day,da.da_mon,da.da_year);
getch();
return 0;
}
```

www.ingramcontent.com/pod-product-compliance
Ingram Content Group UK Ltd.
Pitfield, Milton Keynes, MK11 3LW, UK
UKHW021712190726
13853UKWH00001B/500

9 798886 847505